easy baking

easy baking

simple recipes for cakes, biscuits, pies and breads

Linda Collister

RYLAND
PETERS
& SMALL

LONDON NEW YORK

Designer Luana Gobbo

Commissioning Editor
Elsa Petersen-Schepelern

Editor Sharon Ashman

Production Paul Harding

Art Director Gabriella Le Grazie

Publishing Director Alison Starling

For Alan

First published as *Linda Collister's Baking Bible*
in Great Britain in 2004

This paperback edition published in 2008
by Ryland Peters & Small
20–21 Jockey's Fields
London WC1R 4BW
www.rylandpeters.com

10 9 8 7 6 5 4 3 2 1

ISBN 978 1 84597 746 7

A CIP record for this book is available from the
British Library.

Printed in China

Notes:
Ovens should be preheated to the specified temperature
– if using a fan-assisted oven, adjust the time and
temperature according to the manufacturer's instructions.

All spoon measurements are level unless otherwise
specified. One teaspoon is 5 ml, 1 tablespoon is 15 ml.

Uncooked egg yolks should not be served to the very
young, the ill or elderly, or to pregnant women.

Most of the breads in this book can be frozen for up
to 1 month. The exceptions are Bacon and Walnut
Fougasses (page 186) Cherry Tomato Focaccia with
Basil (page 191) and Rye and Caraway Loaf (page 202),
which should not be frozen.

The recipes in this book have previously been
published by Ryland Peters & Small as *Chocolate
Baking*, *Sweet Tarts and Pies*, *Cookies, Biscuits and
Biscotti* and *Flavoured Breads*.

contents

the joy of baking

Why bother baking at home when the supermarkets are desperate to sell you ready-made breads, cakes and biscuits?

Because nothing beats the real thing, home made: an honest sponge cake that tastes of real, good butter and fresh eggs; pastry that truly melts in the mouth; bread with flavour, a good texture and chewy crust; biscuits reeking of real vanilla; intense pure chocolate desserts. The fact is that quality ingredients result in high quality flavour.

For me, baking combines so many pleasures: the creative pride of making something, social satisfaction in the sharing of my spoils and the sensual delight in the eating. My recipes are made for sharing.

Obviously to use this book you need an oven and you cannot bake well without a good, controllable one. I've used a lot of ovens over the years, from bottled gas stoves in remote log cabins to ultra-modern, top-of-the-range appliances, from solid fuel iron ranges to wood-fired brick ovens. As a result, I have found that an oven thermometer is an essential piece of equipment. Thermostats are often unreliable and you need to know how your oven behaves, so get an inexpensive thermometer and check your oven. The cooking times given in this book are guidelines; your oven handbook and your experience will teach you which shelf works best for you.

If you do a lot of baking, heavy-duty professional-quality tins and trays are a good investment. They will not buckle or scorch in the oven or rust after washing and should last a lifetime. Non-stick baking paper is particularly useful for lining baking sheets when making meringues or delicate biscuits and a large wire cooling rack is very convenient for everything from biscuits to bread.

The two other pieces of equipment I use most are a large, free-standing electric mixer, which makes cake batter, whisks egg whites and kneads bread dough, and a food processor. Hard though this is to admit, these days I would not make pastry without a food processor – my machine does a far better job than my hands.

Have fun – bake something simple and irresistible.

chocolate
baking

the food of the gods

Eating chocolate is pure joy, cooking with it a delight, even smelling it bewitching, but buying it shakes my faith in human nature. The best chocolate is wonderful, but most is not worth buying and most people buy terrible stuff. Good quality plain or dark chocolate will taste smooth not greasy, bitter not raw, intense not oversweet, with a long finish, not a cloying aftertaste.

But how do you know good quality? Price is not a reliable guide – in fact supermarkets' own brands are usually excellent and are a good bargain when buying in bulk for cooking.

The quality and taste of chocolate is determined by the quantity and quality of the cocoa solids – the dry solids plus the added cocoa butter – used in its production. The quantity of solids, at least, is indicated on the packet. Couverture chocolate, used for fillings and icings, has around 55 per cent cocoa solids; bitter chocolate around 65 per cent; and super amer or extra bitter, plain chocolate, best for puddings, fine cakes and eating, has just over 70 per cent. Some chocolates labelled 'for cooking' can contain as little as 30 per cent cocoa solids: the rest is sugar, fats and flavourings.

The raw material for chocolate is the cocoa bean, found in the large yellow-green fruits of the *Theobroma cacao* tree which grows only within 20 degrees north or south of the equator. Each tree yields enough beans to make around 2.5 kg of chocolate each year. The best chocolate is made from a blend of beans – each type has its own individual character and colour ranging from pale coffee through to dark mahogany brown.

Store chocolate well away from other foods in an airtight container in a cool, dry place, because it can easily be tainted by other flavours. Avoid storing chocolate below 13°C, or in the fridge, as beads of moisture will form when it returns to room temperature.

Don't store in a hot kitchen (30°C or above) or it will develop a white bloom as the cocoa butter comes to the surface. The bloom doesn't affect its taste however – it can still be used for cooking. Chocolate begins melting at 30°C (that's why it melts in the mouth) and burns at 110°C.

Melt it slowly and gradually as it easily becomes overheated and scorched, and turns into an unusable solid mass. Chop it into evenly sized pieces so it melts at the same rate. Put it in a shallow, heatproof bowl set over a pan of steaming hot, not boiling, water. The water must not touch the base of the bowl and no drop of water or steam should touch the chocolate or it will seize up. Stir frequently. Remove the bowl from the heat as soon as the chocolate melts.

CHOCOLATE CAKES

almond chocolate kugelhopf

400 g strong white bread flour

½ teaspoon sea salt

15 g fresh yeast*

60 g golden caster sugar

200 ml skimmed milk, lukewarm

3 medium eggs, beaten

100 g unsalted butter, softened

50 g slivered or flaked almonds

60 g plain chocolate, roughly chopped

icing sugar, for dusting

Nut Coating

25 g unsalted butter, very soft

50 g slivered or flaked almonds

a kugelhopf mould, 23 cm diameter

Makes 1 large cake

*To use easy-blend dried yeast, mix one 7 g sachet with 140 g of the flour. Mix in the sugar and milk and let rise for 30 minutes. Make a well in the remaining flour, add the salt, yeast liquid and eggs and proceed with the recipe.

To make the nut coating, thickly butter the inside of the kugelhopf mould with the very soft butter, then press the almonds all around. Chill while preparing the dough.

To make the dough, put the flour and salt in a large bowl and mix, then make a well in the centre.

Crumble the yeast into a small bowl, add the sugar and milk, then cream to a smooth liquid. Pour into the well in the flour and work in enough flour to make a thick batter.

Cover with a damp tea towel and leave at normal room temperature for 30 minutes. The batter should look bubbly. Add the eggs to the yeast liquid, stir until mixed, then gradually beat in the flour to make a soft and very sticky dough. Beat the dough in the bowl with your hand or with the dough hook in an electric mixer for about 5 minutes or until it becomes firmer, smooth, very elastic and shiny.

Work in the softened butter until thoroughly mixed, then add the almonds and chocolate. When evenly mixed, carefully spoon the soft dough into the prepared mould (it should be half full).

Cover the mould with a damp tea towel and let rise at normal room temperature until the dough has almost doubled in size and has risen to about 2.5 cm below the rim of the mould. This should take about 1 hour.

Bake in a preheated oven at 200°C (400°F) Gas 6 for about 45 minutes, or until the cake is golden brown and a skewer inserted into the dough midway between the outer edge and inner tube comes out clean. Remove from the oven and let cool in the mould for 1 minute, then carefully unmould the cake. Transfer to a wire rack to cool completely. Serve dusted with icing sugar.

Store in an airtight container and eat within 3 days, or freeze for up to 1 month. It can also be lightly toasted under a grill.

VARIATIONS

Marbled Kugelhopf Replace 50 g of the strong white bread flour with 50 g sieved cocoa powder and 25 g sugar. Replace the 60 g plain chocolate with a similar quantity of white chocolate, roughly chopped. Proceed as in the main recipe.

Sultana Kugelhopf Replace 50 g of the strong white bread flour with 50 g sieved cocoa powder and 25 g sugar. Replace the 60 g plain chocolate with a similar quantity of sultanas or raisins. Proceed as in the main recipe.

NOTE: Both cocoa variations of this recipe are delicious toasted and spread with butter or peanut butter.

This pretty, yeast coffee-time cake is made in a traditional earthenware mould, a tube pan or non-stick ring mould. Serve it either plain or toasted.

chocolate gingerbread

A great combination of bitter chocolate and ginger in syrup.

Melt the chocolate very gently in a heatproof bowl set over a pan of steaming, not boiling, water. Stir until smooth, remove the bowl from the heat and let cool. Using an electric mixer or wooden spoon, beat the butter until creamy, then gradually beat in the sugar. Beat until light and fluffy, then beat in the egg yolks one at a time, beating well after each addition.

Beat in the cooled chocolate, then sift the almonds, flour and cocoa into the bowl. Add the 3 pieces chopped ginger and syrup and fold in gently using a large metal spoon.

In a separate bowl, whisk the egg whites until stiff peaks form, then fold them into the chocolate mixture in 3 batches.

Spoon the mixture into the prepared tin and smooth the surface. Bake in a preheated oven at 190°C (375°F) Gas 5 for about 40 minutes or until a skewer inserted into the centre of the cake comes out clean. Remove from the oven, let cool in the tin for 5 minutes, then carefully unmould and transfer to a wire rack to cool completely.

To make the topping, melt the chocolate, butter and syrup in a heatproof bowl set over a pan of steaming, not boiling, water. Stir until smooth, then spoon over the top of the cake. When almost set, decorate with finely sliced or grated stem ginger.

Store in an airtight container and eat within 1 week – the flavour improves after several days. If undecorated, it can be frozen for up to 1 month.

150 g plain chocolate, chopped

150 g unsalted butter, at room temperature

150 g golden caster sugar

3 large eggs, separated

50 g ground almonds

120 g self-raising flour

1 tablespoon cocoa powder

3 pieces stem ginger, chopped, plus 1 piece stem ginger, finely sliced or grated, to finish

2 tablespoons syrup from jar of stem ginger

Chocolate Topping

40 g plain chocolate, chopped

15 g unsalted butter

1 tablespoon syrup from jar of stem ginger

a loaf tin, 22 x 11 x 7 cm, greased and base-lined

Makes 1 cake

marbled fudge cake

This cake improves in flavour for several days after baking.

To make the base, put the biscuit crumbs and melted butter in a bowl and mix well. Press the mixture into the base of the springform pan to make a thin, even layer. Chill while preparing the filling.

To make the chocolate mixture, melt the chocolate gently in a heatproof bowl set over a pan of steaming, not boiling, water. Stir until smooth, remove the bowl from the heat and stir in the butter.

In another bowl beat the eggs and sugar with a wooden spoon until frothy. Sift the flour, salt and baking powder into the bowl and stir well. Add the chocolate and butter mixture and the vanilla essence. Chop the nuts, add to the bowl and mix well. Spread the mixture over the base.

To make the vanilla mixture, bring the butter to room temperature, then beat until creamy using a wooden spoon or electric mixer. Beat in the vanilla essence and cream cheese until the mixture is light and fluffy. Gradually beat in the sugar, then the egg. Add the flour and stir well.

Spoon the mixture on top of the chocolate layer in the pan. Swirl the tip of a knife through both mixtures to give a marbled effect.

Bake in a preheated oven at 180°C (350°F) Gas 4 for about 25 minutes until just firm. Remove from the oven and let cool in the pan before unmoulding. Serve at room temperature.

Store in an airtight container and eat within 5 days, or freeze for up to 1 month.

80 g digestive biscuits, crushed

50 g unsalted butter, melted

Chocolate Mixture

120 g plain chocolate, chopped

35 g unsalted butter, diced, at room temperature

2 large eggs

150 g golden caster sugar

75 g plain flour

a pinch of salt

½ teaspoon baking powder

2–3 drops real vanilla essence

50 g walnut or pecan pieces

Vanilla Mixture

25 g unsalted butter

½ teaspoon real vanilla essence

85 g Philadelphia cream cheese

50 g golden caster sugar

1 large egg, beaten

10 g plain flour

a springform pan, 21 cm diameter, greased

Makes 1 cake (16 slices)

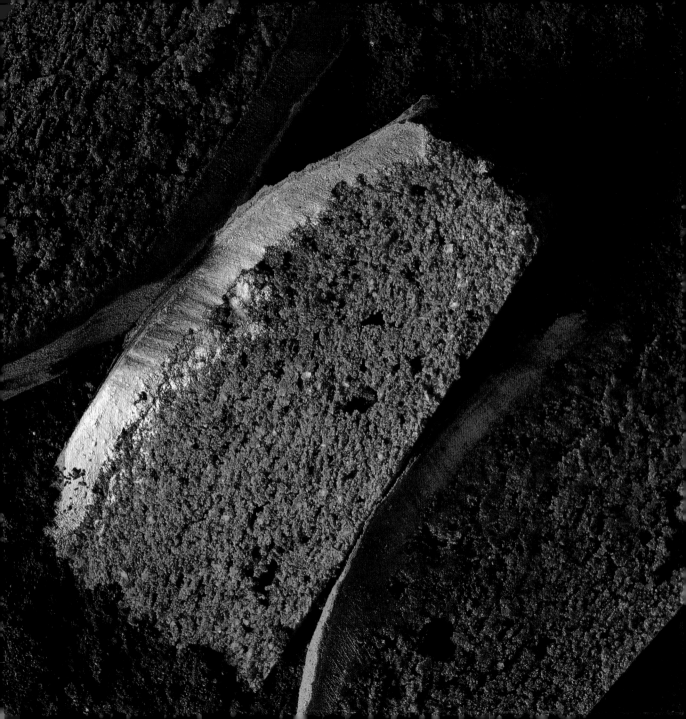

espresso cake

225 g self-raising flour

90 g cocoa powder

a pinch of salt

1 tablespoon very finely ground espresso coffee

120 g ground almonds

230 g unsalted butter

230 g golden caster sugar

4 large eggs, beaten

3 tablespoons very hot water

1 tablespoon coffee liqueur or brandy (optional)

Chocolate Icing

150 ml double cream (not the extra-thick kind)

150 g plain chocolate, chopped

1 tablespoon very strong black coffee, coffee liqueur or brandy

a springform pan, 24 cm diameter, greased and base-lined

Makes 1 cake

Finely ground espresso coffee rather than liquid coffee may appear to be a rather odd ingredient for this moist cake – but it tastes extraordinarily good!

Sift the flour, cocoa, salt, coffee and ground almonds together into a bowl.

In a separate bowl, beat the butter until creamy using a wooden spoon or electric mixer. Gradually beat in the sugar until light and fluffy, then beat in the eggs, 1 tablespoon at a time.

Carefully fold in the dry ingredients using a large metal spoon, then stir in the hot water and coffee liqueur or brandy, if using. Gently spoon the mixture into the prepared springform pan and smooth the surface. Bake in a preheated oven at 180°C (350°F) Gas 4 for about 40 minutes or until a skewer inserted into the centre comes out clean. Remove from the oven, carefully loosen the cake, then unclip the pan. Transfer to a wire rack to cool.

To make the icing, heat the cream until scalding hot, then remove from the heat and add the chocolate and coffee or alcohol. Leave until completely melted, then stir gently.

When cool and thick enough to spread, use to cover the top and sides of the cake. Leave until set, then store in an airtight container overnight before cutting.

Eat within 1 week, or freeze for up to 1 month.

fudgy nut cake

350 g plain chocolate, chopped

175 g unsalted butter, diced

55 g cocoa powder, sifted, plus extra for dusting

5 large eggs

1 teaspoon real vanilla essence

250 g golden caster sugar

100 g mixed nuts, roughly chopped

icing sugar, for dusting

a springform pan, 22 cm diameter, greased and base-lined

Makes 1 cake

Make this soft, moist, flourless cake with a mixture of nuts, such as macadamias, pecans, walnuts, almonds or hazelnuts.

Put the chopped chocolate and diced butter in a heatproof bowl set over a pan of steaming, not boiling, water. Stir frequently until melted and smooth. Remove the bowl from the heat, stir in the cocoa and let cool.

Meanwhile, put the eggs, vanilla essence and sugar in a large heatproof bowl and whisk briefly until frothy. Set the bowl over a pan of steaming water – the water should not touch the base of the bowl. Using an electric hand whisk, whisk the mixture until it is very pale and thick – when the whisk is lifted it should leave a visible ribbon-like trail.

Remove the bowl from the heat, and whisk for a couple of minutes so the mixture cools. Using a large metal spoon, carefully fold in the cooled chocolate mixture, followed by the nuts. When thoroughly combined, spoon the mixture into the prepared springform pan and smooth the surface.

Bake in a preheated oven at 180°C (350°F) Gas 4 for about 35 minutes or until firm to the touch but moist inside (do not overcook or the cake will be dry and hard to slice).

Remove from the oven and let cool in the pan. Unclip the pan, turn out the cake and serve, dusted with icing sugar and cocoa. Store in an airtight container and eat within 1 week. It does not freeze well.

chocolate pound cake

Rum-soaked sultanas, butter, sugar, flour and cocoa – a terrific combination. Don't worry if the fruit sinks during baking.

70 g sultanas

3 tablespoons rum

250 g unsalted butter, at room temperature

250 g golden caster sugar

4 large eggs, at room temperature

50 g cocoa powder

200 g self-raising flour

a pinch of salt

a loaf tin, 900 g, lined with a double thickness of greaseproof paper, greased

Makes 1 large cake

Soak the sultanas in the rum, cover and set aside overnight.

Put the soft butter in the bowl of an electric mixer and beat until creamy. Gradually beat in the sugar. After the last addition beat the mixture until it becomes very pale and light in texture.

Put the eggs in a separate bowl and beat. Add to the butter mixture, 1 tablespoon at a time, beating well after each addition.

Sift the cocoa, flour and salt twice, then add to the egg mixture. Fold in the dry ingredients very gently using a large metal spoon. When thoroughly combined, fold in the sultanas and any rum left in the bowl.

Spoon the mixture into the prepared tin and smooth the surface. Bake in a preheated oven at 200°C (400°F) Gas 6 for 40–50 minutes or until a cocktail stick or skewer inserted into the centre of the cake comes out clean.

Let the cake cool in the tin for a couple of minutes, then lift it out and peel off the paper. Transfer to a wire rack to cool completely.

Store in an airtight container and eat within 1 week, or freeze up to 1 month.

devil's food cake

An unusual, quick and easy method that produces a very dark cake – yet light and full of flavour.

Put the chocolate, butter, sugar and syrup in a heavy saucepan. Heat very gently, stirring frequently until melted. Remove the pan from the heat and let cool.

Sift the flour, cocoa and bicarbonate of soda into a large bowl and make a well in the centre. Pour in the melted chocolate mixture, stir gently, then add the eggs, vanilla essence and milk. Beat very gently with a wooden spoon until well mixed.

Spoon the mixture into the prepared tins and spread evenly. Bake in a preheated oven at 170°C (325°F) Gas 3 for 15–20 minutes until just firm to the touch. Remove from the oven and let cool in the tins for 5 minutes, then turn out and transfer to a wire rack to cool completely.

To make the icing, put the milk and sugar in a saucepan. Heat gently, stirring frequently until the sugar has dissolved, then boil rapidly for 1 minute until syrupy. Remove the pan from the heat and stir in the chocolate. When melted and smooth, stir in the butter and vanilla essence. Let cool, stirring occasionally, then beat well until very thick.

Spread one-third of the icing on to one of the cakes. Set the second layer on top. Spread the rest of the mixture evenly over the top and sides. Leave in a cool spot (not the refrigerator) until set. Store in an airtight container and eat within 5 days. The undecorated cakes can be frozen for up to 1 month.

90+60 = 150g plain chocolate

90 g plain chocolate, chopped

115 g unsalted butter

90 g dark muscovado sugar

1 tablespoon golden syrup

175 g plain flour

25 g cocoa powder

½ teaspoon bicarbonate of soda

2 large eggs, beaten

½ teaspoon real vanilla essence

90 ml whole milk

Chocolate Icing

150 ml whole milk

100 g golden caster sugar

60 g plain chocolate, chopped

60 g unsalted butter, at room temperature

½ teaspoon real vanilla essence

2 sandwich tins, 18 cm diameter, greased and base-lined

Makes 1 cake

CHOCOLATE BISCUITS

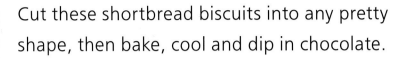

cinnamon chocolate stars

180 g unsalted butter, at room temperature

90 g golden caster sugar

230 g plain flour

a good pinch of salt

1 teaspoon ground cinnamon

40 g rice flour, ground rice or cornflour

50 g plain chocolate, to finish

a medium star-shaped cutter

several baking sheets, greased

Makes about 30

Cut these shortbread biscuits into any pretty shape, then bake, cool and dip in chocolate.

Using a wooden spoon or electric mixer, beat the butter until creamy. Gradually beat in the sugar. When the mixture is pale and fluffy, sift the flour, salt, cinnamon and rice flour, ground rice or cornflour into the bowl and mix. When the mixture comes together, turn it out on to a lightly floured work surface and knead lightly and briefly to make a smooth, but not sticky dough. In hot weather, or if the dough feels sticky, wrap and chill until firm.

Roll out the dough to about 5 mm thick and cut out shapes with the cutter. Gently knead together the trimmings, then re-roll and cut more stars.

Arrange the stars on the prepared baking sheets, spaced slightly apart. Prick with a fork and chill for about 15 minutes.

Bake the biscuits in a preheated oven at 180°C (350°F) Gas 4 for 12–15 minutes or until firm and barely coloured.

Remove from the oven and let cool on the baking sheets for a couple of minutes until firm enough to transfer to a wire rack to cool completely.

When the biscuits are completely cold, melt the chocolate gently in a small heatproof bowl set over a saucepan of steaming, not boiling, water. Stir until smooth, then remove the bowl from the heat. Dip the points of the stars in the melted chocolate, then leave to set on waxed paper, non-stick parchment or a wire rack.

When firm, store in an airtight container and eat within 3 days. Undecorated biscuits can be frozen for up to 1 month.

chocolate crackles

These biscuits crack and spread in the oven – finish them off with a dusting of icing sugar to make them look even more dramatic.

Melt the chopped chocolate gently in a heatproof bowl set over a saucepan of steaming, not boiling, water, stirring frequently. Remove the bowl from the heat and gradually stir in the butter. In a separate bowl, whisk the egg and vanilla essence until frothy using a wire whisk or electric mixer. Gradually whisk in the sugar, followed by the melted chocolate mixture.

Sift the flour and bicarbonate of soda into the bowl, then stir in to make a firm dough. In hot weather, or if the dough seems sticky, wrap and chill for 15 minutes.

Using your hands, roll the dough into walnut-sized balls. Roll each ball in icing sugar, then arrange on the prepared baking sheets spacing them well apart.

Bake in a preheated oven at 200°C (400°F) Gas 6 for 10–12 minutes until just firm. Remove from the oven and let cool on the baking sheets for 1 minute until firm enough to transfer to a wire rack to cool completely.

Store in an airtight container and eat within 1 week, or freeze for up to 1 month.

115 g plain chocolate, roughly chopped

115 g unsalted butter, diced, at room temperature

1 large egg

2–3 drops real vanilla essence

175 g light brown muscovado sugar

175 g self-raising flour

½ teaspoon bicarbonate of soda

about 2 tablespoons icing sugar, for coating

several baking sheets, greased

Makes about 28

Only the finest chocolate is suitable for this recipe.

bitter chocolate butter biscuits

70 g plain chocolate, roughly chopped (preferably with at least 70 per cent cocoa solids and very little sugar)

35 g golden caster sugar

220 g unsalted butter, chilled and diced

140 g light brown muscovado sugar

250 g plain flour

½ teaspoon real vanilla essence

50 g white or plain chocolate, melted, to finish

several baking sheets, well greased

Makes 30

Put the chopped chocolate and caster sugar in a food processor and process until they form the texture of sand. Add the diced butter, sugar, flour and vanilla essence, then process again just until the dough comes together.

Using your hands, form the dough into about 30 walnut-sized balls. Arrange them on the prepared baking sheets, spacing them well apart.

Bake the biscuits in a preheated oven at 180°C (350°F) Gas 4 for 10–15 minutes or until they are just firm to the touch and beginning to colour around the edges.

Remove from the oven. They are very fragile at this stage, so leave them on the sheets for 5 minutes to firm up before transferring to a wire rack to cool.

When the biscuits are completely cold, decorate by drizzling with the melted chocolate using either a fork or a greaseproof paper icing bag. Let set.

Store in an airtight container and eat within 4 days. Undecorated biscuits can be frozen for up to 1 month, but you may have to crisp them in a warm oven before decorating.

black and white biscuits

115 g unsalted butter, at room temperature

85 g light brown muscovado sugar

1 large egg, beaten

60 g self-raising flour

½ teaspoon baking powder

a pinch of salt

½ teaspoon real vanilla essence

115 g porridge oats

175 g plain chocolate, chopped into chunks

several baking sheets, greased

Makes about 24

Make chocolate chips by chopping a bar of good plain chocolate into large chunks – the flavour is far superior to commercial chocolate chips.

Using a wooden spoon or electric mixer, beat the butter until creamy. Add the sugar and beat until light and fluffy. Gradually beat in the egg, beating well after the last addition. Sift the flour, baking powder and salt into the mixture, add the vanilla essence and oats and stir in. When thoroughly mixed, stir in the chocolate chunks.

Put heaped teaspoons of the mixture, spaced well apart, on the prepared sheets. Bake in a preheated oven at 180°C (350°F) Gas 4 for 12–15 minutes until golden and just firm. Remove from the oven and let cool on the sheets for a couple of minutes until firm enough to transfer to a wire rack to cool completely.

Store in an airtight container. Eat within 1 week, or freeze for up to 1 month.

Chocolate chip biscuits with a difference – the dough is flavoured with melted chocolate as well as chunks of plain chocolate.

giant double chocolate nut biscuits

Put the 140 g chocolate in a heatproof bowl and gently melt over a saucepan of steaming, not boiling, water. Remove the bowl from the heat and let cool.

Meanwhile, beat the butter until creamy using a wooden spoon or electric mixer. Add the sugars and beat again until light and fluffy. Gradually beat in the egg and vanilla essence, followed by the melted chocolate.

Sift the flour, salt and baking powder into the mixture and stir. When thoroughly mixed, stir in the chopped nuts and chocolate chunks.

Put heaped tablespoons of the dough, spaced well apart, on the prepared baking sheets.

Bake in a preheated oven at 180°C (350°F) Gas 4 for 12–15 minutes until just firm. Remove from the oven and let cool on the baking sheets for a couple of minutes until firm enough to transfer to a wire rack to cool completely.

Store in an airtight container. Eat within 1 week, or freeze for up to 1 month.

140 g plain chocolate, chopped

100 g unsalted butter, at room temperature

80 g golden caster sugar

80 g dark brown muscovado sugar

1 large egg, beaten

½ teaspoon real vanilla essence

150 g plain flour

a pinch of salt

½ teaspoon baking powder

50 g pecans or walnuts, chopped

100 g plain dark (or white) chocolate, chopped into chunks

several baking sheets, greased

Makes 16

TEACAKES
& SQUARES

squillionaire's shortbread

397 g canned condensed milk

**120 g unsalted butter,
at room temperature**

60 g golden caster sugar

160 g plain flour

20 g cocoa powder

Chocolate Topping

160 g plain chocolate, chopped

30 g unsalted butter, chopped

**about 50 g white chocolate,
to finish**

*a cake tin, 20 cm square and
5 cm deep, greased*

Makes 16

Put the unopened can of condensed milk in a heavy saucepan and cover with water. Bring to the boil, then simmer without covering the pan for 3½ hours. Top up the water regularly: the can must always be covered with water. Let the can cool completely before opening. The condensed milk should have become a fudgy, dark, golden caramel.

Meanwhile, to make the chocolate biscuit base, beat the butter using a wooden spoon or electric mixer until creamy. Beat in the sugar until the mixture is light and fluffy. Sift the flour with the cocoa into the bowl and work with your hands to make a smooth dough. Press the dough into the prepared cake tin to make an even layer. Prick well with a fork and chill for 15 minutes.

Bake the biscuit base in a preheated oven at 180°C (350°F) Gas 4 for 20 minutes until just firm and very slightly darker around the edges – do not overcook or it will taste bitter. Remove from the oven and let cool in the tin. When completely cold, spread the cold caramel over the top. Chill until firm – 1–2 hours.

To make the chocolate topping, melt the plain chocolate gently in a heatproof bowl set over a saucepan of steaming, not boiling, water. Remove the bowl from the heat and stir in the butter. When smooth, spread over the caramel and let set. Melt the white chocolate in the same way, then drizzle it over the top of the plain chocolate using a fork or a greaseproof paper icing bag.

Leave overnight until firm before cutting. Store in an airtight container and eat within 1 week. Not suitable for freezing.

three-chocolate squares

Three kinds of chocolate – white, plain and cocoa – make great little cakes, which are perfect with a cup of coffee.

Melt the plain chocolate gently in a heatproof bowl set over a saucepan of steaming, not boiling, water. Stir occasionally. Remove the bowl from the heat and let cool.

Meanwhile, beat the butter until creamy using a wooden spoon or electric mixer. Add the sugar and vanilla essence and beat well. Gradually beat in the egg, followed by the cooled chocolate.

Sift the flour with the baking powder, bicarbonate of soda and cocoa into a separate bowl. Using a metal spoon, fold the flour mixture into the chocolate mixture in 3 batches, alternating with the soured cream. When thoroughly mixed, spoon into the prepared cake tin and smooth the surface.

Bake in a preheated oven at 190°C (375°F) Gas 5 until just firm – 25–30 minutes. Remove from the oven and let cool in the tin before turning out.

To make the topping, melt the white chocolate in the same way as the plain chocolate above, then stir in the butter. When smooth, spread over the cake and let set. Cut into 16 pieces and store in an airtight container. Eat within 5 days, or freeze for up to 1 month.

60 g plain chocolate, chopped

120 g unsalted butter, at room temperature

170 g light brown muscovado sugar

½ teaspoon real vanilla essence

1 large egg, beaten

220 g plain flour

1 teaspoon baking powder

½ teaspoon bicarbonate of soda

25 g cocoa powder

150 ml soured cream

White Chocolate Topping

50 g good quality white chocolate, chopped

20 g unsalted butter, at room temperature

a cake tin, 20 cm square, greased and base-lined

Makes 16

fudge brownies

A wonderful version of one of the great American classics.

140 g unsalted butter

4 large eggs, beaten

340 g light brown muscovado sugar

1 teaspoon real vanilla essence

a good pinch of salt

75 g cocoa powder

140 g plain flour

100 g walnut or pecan pieces, white or plain chocolate, chopped, or a combination

a cake tin, 23 cm square and 5 cm deep, completely lined with foil

Makes 16

Put the butter in a saucepan and heat gently until melted. Let cool while preparing the rest of the mixture.

Using a wooden spoon, beat the eggs very gently with the sugar until just blended and free of lumps. Stir in the cooled butter and the vanilla essence. Sift the salt, cocoa and flour together into the butter mixture and gently stir in – do not beat or overmix, or the brownies will become cake-like.

When mixed, fold in the nuts and/or chocolate. Spoon into the prepared cake tin and smooth the surface.

Bake in a preheated oven at 170°C (325°F) Gas 3 for 35–40 minutes or until a skewer inserted midway between the centre and the side of the tin comes out clean. The centre should be just firm – do not overcook or the brownies will be dry.

Remove from the oven and put the tin on a damp tea towel to cool completely.

When cool, lift the cake, still in the foil, out of the tin. Remove the foil and cut the brownies into 16 squares.

Store in an airtight container and eat within 1 week, or freeze for up to 1 month.

blondies

These pale-gold brownies are topped with chopped walnuts and two kinds of chocolate – dark and white.

Put the butter in a large, heavy saucepan and heat gently until melted. Add the sugar, stir well, then remove the pan from the heat. Let cool for 1 minute, then stir in the vanilla essence and the eggs.

Sift the flour, baking powder and salt into the pan and stir just until thoroughly blended – do not beat or overmix.

Spoon the mixture into the prepared tin and smooth the surface. Sprinkle the nuts and chopped chocolate over the top.

Bake in a preheated oven at 180°C (350°F) Gas 4 for about 25 minutes until just firm.

Remove from the oven and let cool for a few minutes in the tin, then lift the cake, still in the foil, on to a wire rack to cool completely.

Remove the foil and cut the blondies into 48 squares. Store in an airtight container and eat within 4 days. They can be frozen for up to 1 month, but they will be stickier than freshly baked ones.

140 g unsalted butter

400 g light brown muscovado sugar

1 teaspoon real vanilla essence

3 large eggs, beaten

300 g plain flour

1 teaspoon baking powder

a large pinch of salt

50 g walnut pieces, roughly chopped

50 g good-quality white chocolate, roughly chopped

50 g plain chocolate, roughly chopped

a roasting or baking tin, 30 x 22 cm, lined with foil

Makes 48

mocha madeleines

140 g unsalted butter, diced,
at room temperature

85 g plain chocolate, chopped

140 g plain flour

2 tablespoons cocoa powder

a pinch of salt

1 teaspoon finely ground
espresso coffee

4 large eggs

140 g golden caster sugar

icing sugar, for dusting

madeleine moulds, twice buttered*

Makes 30

**Non-stick moulds work best. If
using ordinary metal moulds, brush
with 2 coats of melted butter and
chill between applications.*

A delicate mixture flavoured with finely ground coffee.

Melt the butter and chocolate gently in a heatproof bowl set over a saucepan of steaming, not boiling, water, stirring frequently. Remove the bowl from the heat and let cool.

Meanwhile, sift the flour twice with the cocoa, salt and coffee, then set aside. Put the eggs and sugar in a separate bowl and whisk using an electric mixer until the mixture becomes pale and thick – when the whisk is lifted out the mixture should leave a ribbon-like trail on the surface.

Using a large metal spoon, fold the flour mixture into the egg mixture in 3 batches, then carefully fold in the chocolate mixture until all are thoroughly combined (the mixture will lose a little bulk).

Put a heaped teaspoon or so of the mixture into each madeleine mould so it is two-thirds full.

Bake in a preheated oven at 190°C (375°F) Gas 5 for 10–12 minutes or until just firm.

Remove from the oven and let cool for 1 minute, then carefully remove the madeleines from the moulds using a round-bladed knife. Transfer to a wire rack to cool completely, then dust with icing sugar.

Store in an airtight container and eat within 1 week, or freeze for up to 1 month.

CHOCOLATE
TARTS & PIES

chocolate pear tart

To make the pastry, sift the flour into a bowl, then rub in the diced butter with the tips of your fingers until the mixture resembles fine crumbs.

Stir in the sugar, add the egg yolk and water, then bind the mixture together using a pastry-blender or round-bladed knife. If the dough is dry and crumbly, add a little extra water, 1 tablespoon at a time. Without kneading, quickly bring the dough together with your hands to make a soft but not sticky ball.

To make the pastry in a food processor, put the flour, butter and sugar in the bowl and process until the mixture resembles fine crumbs. With the machine running, add the egg yolk and water through the feed tube and process just until the dough comes together.

Wrap the dough and chill it for 20 minutes. Roll out the pastry on a lightly floured work surface to a circle about 29 cm across and use to line the flan tin. Chill while preparing the filling.

Put a baking sheet in a preheated oven at 200°C (400°F) Gas 6 to heat up – this helps to make the pastry base crisp.

To make the filling, melt the chocolate very gently in a heatproof bowl set over a saucepan of steaming, not boiling, water. Stir until smooth, then remove the bowl from the heat and let cool.

Meanwhile, using an electric mixer or wooden spoon, beat the butter until creamy, then beat in the sugar. When the mixture is light and fluffy, beat in the egg yolks 1 at a time, beating well after each addition. Beat in the cooled chocolate, then stir in the ground almonds and essence using a large metal spoon.

180 g plain flour

110 g unsalted butter, chilled and diced

35 g golden caster sugar

1 egg yolk

about 1 tablespoon iced water

crème fraîche or vanilla ice cream, to serve

Chocolate Pear Filling
125 g plain chocolate, chopped

125 g unsalted butter, at room temperature

90 g golden caster sugar

4 large eggs, separated

125 g ground almonds

2–3 drops real almond essence

a pinch of salt

2 ripe medium pears

a deep, loose-based flan tin, 23 cm diameter

a baking sheet

Makes 1 tart, serves 8

In a spotlessly clean, grease-free bowl, whisk the egg whites with the pinch of salt until they form soft peaks. Using a large metal spoon, gently fold them into the chocolate mixture in 3 batches. Gently spoon into the prepared chilled pastry case and smooth the surface.

Peel and halve the pears, then scoop out the cores with a melon-baller or pointed teaspoon. Thinly slice the pear halves, leaving the slices attached at the stalk end, so they resemble fans. Arrange the pears on top of the chocolate mixture in a neat pattern.

Set the flan tin on the heated baking sheet and bake for 15 minutes. Reduce the oven temperature to 180°C (350°F) Gas 4 and bake for about 10 minutes longer or until the tart is just cooked in the centre – test by piercing the filling with a skewer, it should come out clean.

Remove from the oven and very carefully unmould the tart. Serve either warm or at room temperature with crème fraîche or vanilla ice cream. The tart tastes better the day after baking, though it sinks slightly.

VARIATION

Chocolate Normandy Tart

Substitute crisp, tart eating apples for the pears and prepare them in the same way. Add ½ teaspoon ground cinnamon to the chocolate filling, and proceed as in the main recipe.

Use just-ripe Comice pears for this rich, not-too-sweet tart.

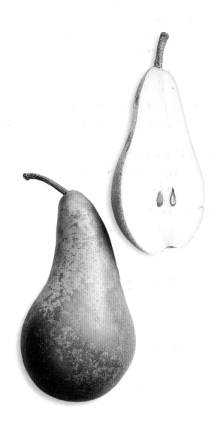

chestnut and chocolate moneybags

about 300 g filo pastry

250 g curd cheese

40 g dark muscovado sugar

2 medium egg yolks

2–3 tablespoons rum

200 g plain chocolate, coarsely grated

120 g drained cooked chestnuts, roughly chopped (vacuum packed or canned in light syrup or water)

60 g unsalted butter, melted, for brushing

icing sugar, for dusting

several baking sheets

Makes 12, serves 4–6

If necessary, defrost the pastry according to the packet instructions.

To make the filling, beat the curd cheese until softened using a wooden spoon, then beat in the sugar followed by the egg yolks. Add rum to taste. Using a metal spoon, gently stir in the grated chocolate and the chestnuts.

Remove the pastry from its packaging and cover with a damp tea towel until ready to use – the sheets of dough dry out very easily and become unusable.

Put 3 sheets of the pastry on top of each other on a work surface and cut into 18 cm squares. Put a good tablespoon of the mixture (¹⁄₁₂ of the amount) into the centre of each square, gather up the edges and twist the top to resemble a pastry moneybag. There is no need to dampen the edges of the pastry. Repeat to make 12 pastry bags.

Arrange, spaced well apart, on the baking sheets and chill for 15 minutes.

Brush the pastry with melted butter, then bake in a preheated oven at 190°C (375°F) Gas 5 for about 15 minutes until golden brown. Serve, dusted with icing sugar.

Serve warm, at room temperature, or chilled with vanilla ice cream, crème fraîche or chocolate sauce.

southern deep-dish pecan pie

A pecan pie with nuts, chocolate and
American bourbon.

To make the pastry, put the flour and salt in a food processor. Add the butter and process until the mixture resembles fine crumbs. Add the sugar and process briefly. With the machine running, add the egg yolk and water through the feed tube and process just until the dough comes together. Wrap and chill for 20 minutes until firm.

Roll out the dough on a lightly floured work surface to a large circle about 29 cm across and use to line the flan tin. Prick well and chill for 15 minutes.

To bake the pastry blind, fill with a round of baking parchment and baking beans and cook in a preheated oven at 200°C (400°F) Gas 6 for about 15 minutes until firm. Remove the paper and beans and return the pastry case, still in its tin, to the oven for 5–10 minutes until crisp and golden. Let cool.

To prepare the filling, put the sugar and cream in a heavy saucepan and stir over medium heat until the sugar has melted and the mixture is almost boiling. Remove the pan from the heat and stir in the chocolate. When smooth, add the egg yolks and mix well. Stir over very low heat until the mixture thickens. Remove the pan from the heat and stir in the vanilla essence, bourbon, if using, and nuts. Pour into the prepared pastry case and chill until firm. Serve decorated with white chocolate curls, if using – these are made using a vegetable peeler or grater.

Eat within 3 days. Not suitable for freezing.

180 g plain flour

a pinch of salt

110 g unsalted butter, chilled and diced

35 g caster sugar

1 egg yolk

about 1 tablespoon iced water, to bind

Pecan Filling

220 g light brown muscovado sugar

300 ml double cream

70 g plain chocolate, chopped

2 medium egg yolks

½ teaspoon real vanilla essence

1 tablespoon bourbon (optional)

150 g pecan halves

shaved or grated white chocolate 'curls', to finish (optional)

a deep, loose-based flan tin, 23 cm diameter

Makes 1 pie, serves 8–10

Amaretti add crunchy texture and nutty taste to this easy recipe.

amaretti chocolate cheesecake

To make the crust, put the butter and amaretti crumbs in a bowl and mix, then press on to the base of the prepared pan in an even layer. Chill while making the filling.

To make the filling, melt the chocolate gently in a heatproof bowl set over a saucepan of steaming, not boiling, water. Remove the bowl from the heat, stir until smooth, then let cool.

Put the cream cheese, eggs and sugar in a food processor and process until thoroughly mixed. Add the cream and process again until just mixed. With the machine running, add the melted chocolate and Amaretto, if using, through the feed tube and process until smooth.

Spoon the filling over the crust and smooth the surface. Bake in a preheated oven at 170°C (325°F) Gas 3 for 40 minutes until firm. Let the cheesecake cool in the oven with the door ajar. When completely cold, chill overnight.

Unclip the pan and remove the cheesecake. Decorate the top with the broken amaretti biscuits. Drizzle with melted chocolate using either a greaseproof paper icing bag with the end snipped off or a fork dipped in the chocolate.

Store the cheesecake in a covered container in the refrigerator and remove 30 minutes before serving. Eat within 5 days, or freeze for up to 1 month.

60 g unsalted butter, melted

100 g amaretti biscuits, crushed

Chocolate Filling

200 g plain chocolate, chopped

400 g Philadelphia cream cheese

2 medium eggs

60 g caster sugar

200 ml double cream

50 ml Amaretto liqueur (optional)

To Finish

6 amaretti biscuits, broken

40 g plain chocolate, melted

*a springform pan,
21 cm diameter, greased*

Serves 12

CHOCOLATE PUDDINGS

hot white chocolate pudding

80 g white chocolate, chopped

115 g unsalted butter, at room temperature

115 g golden caster sugar

2 large eggs, beaten

150 g self-raising flour

a pinch of salt

a few drops real vanilla essence

about 3 tablespoons milk

Chocolate Custard

425 ml whole milk

20 g cocoa powder

55 g golden caster sugar

15 g cornflour

2 medium egg yolks

an ovenproof baking dish, 750 ml, well greased

Serves 4

A special cold weather treat – baked white chocolate sponge pudding, served with hot chocolate custard.

Melt the chocolate gently in a heatproof bowl set over a saucepan of steaming, not boiling, water. Remove the bowl from the heat and stir until smooth.

Using a wooden spoon or electric mixer, beat the butter until creamy, then gradually beat in the sugar. When the mixture is very light and fluffy, beat in the eggs, 1 tablespoon at a time, beating well after each addition.

Using a metal spoon, carefully fold in the flour and salt, then fold in the melted chocolate, vanilla essence and enough milk to give a soft, dropping consistency.

Spoon into the prepared dish – it should be two-thirds full. Cover loosely with buttered foil and bake in a preheated oven at 180°C (350°F) Gas 4 for about 35 minutes or until firm.

Meanwhile, to make the chocolate custard, heat the milk in a saucepan until scalding hot. Sift the cocoa, sugar and cornflour into a bowl and mix to a thick paste with the egg yolks and about 1 tablespoon of the hot milk.

Stir in the remaining milk, then return the mixture to the saucepan. Stir over low heat until very hot, thickened and smooth – do not let it boil. Serve immediately with the chocolate pudding.

chocolate rice pudding

A thoroughly self-indulgent, grown-up version of a traditional nursery pudding.

Put the chocolate and milk in a saucepan and heat gently just until melted, stirring occasionally. Remove the pan from the heat and let cool. Put the rice, sugar and vanilla pod in the buttered dish and pour in the chocolate milk.

Stir gently, then bake in a preheated oven at 150°C (300°F) Gas 2 for about 2½ hours until the rice is tender and the pudding has thickened. Serve warm.

VARIATION

Chocolate Rice Cream

This variation is cooked on top of the stove. Omit the vanilla and put the remaining ingredients in a saucepan with 3 green cardamom pods. Bring to the boil, stirring, then simmer for 40 minutes until the rice is soft. Remove the cardamom. Stir in 1 egg yolk and cook for 1 minute. Pour into a large serving dish or individual dishes, let cool, cover and chill. Serve icy cold, sprinkled with icing sugar or a drizzle of cream.

30 g plain chocolate, chopped

550 ml whole milk

35 g round-grain rice

25 g golden caster sugar

1 vanilla pod*

an ovenproof baking dish, 750 ml, very well buttered

Serves 4

*The vanilla pod can be rinsed carefully, dried, then used again.

rich chocolate soufflé

A wonderfully rich, light, smooth soufflé with a surprise filling.

Brush melted butter inside the ramekins and sprinkle with caster sugar. Stand them on a baking sheet or in a roasting tin.

Put the chocolate and cream in a heavy saucepan. Set over very low heat and stir occasionally until melted. Remove the pan from the heat and stir the chocolate mixture gently until smooth. Gently stir in the egg yolks, 1 at a time, then half the brandy or liqueur.

Put the 5 egg whites in a spotlessly clean, grease-free bowl and whisk until stiff peaks form. Sprinkle with the caster sugar and briefly whisk again to make a smooth, stiff meringue. If you over-whisk the meringue at this stage it will do more harm than good and the end result will be less smooth.

The chocolate mixture should be just warm, so gently reheat it if necessary. Using a large metal spoon, mix in a little of the meringue to loosen the consistency, then pour the chocolate mixture on top of the meringue and gently fold together until thoroughly combined but not overmixed.

Half-fill the prepared ramekins with the mixture. Spoon the remaining brandy or liqueur over the amaretti biscuits then put one in the centre of each ramekin. Add the remaining mixture until the ramekins are full almost to the rim.

Bake in a preheated oven at 220°C (425°F) Gas 7 for 8–10 minutes. Remove from the oven when they are barely set (the centres should be soft and wobble when gently shaken). Sprinkle with icing sugar and serve immediately.

170 g plain chocolate, broken into small squares

140 ml double cream

3 medium eggs, separated, plus 2 egg whites

4 tablespoons brandy or Amaretto liqueur

3 tablespoons caster sugar, plus extra for sprinkling

4 amaretti biscuits

melted butter, for brushing

icing sugar, for sprinkling

4 ovenproof ramekins (or similar), 300 ml each

a baking sheet or roasting tin

Serves 4

chocolate terrine

A velvety smooth finale for a special dinner party – serve this terrine with very strong coffee.

Put the chocolate in a heatproof bowl with the cocoa and coffee. Set over a saucepan of steaming, not boiling, water and melt gently, stirring frequently. Remove the bowl from the heat, stir in the brandy and let cool.

Meanwhile, whisk the eggs using an electric mixer until frothy. Add the sugar and whisk until the mixture is pale and very thick – the whisk should leave a ribbon-like trail when lifted.

In a separate bowl, whip the cream until it holds a soft peak. Using a large metal spoon, gently fold the chocolate mixture into the eggs. When well mixed, fold in the whipped cream.

Spoon the mixture into the prepared loaf tin, then stand the tin in a bain-marie (a roasting tin half-filled with warm water).

Bake in a preheated oven at 170°C (325°F) Gas 3 for 1–1¼ hours or until a skewer inserted into the centre of the mixture comes out clean.

Remove from the oven, let cool in the bain-marie for about 45 minutes, then lift the loaf tin out of the bain-marie and let cool completely.

Chill overnight, then turn out. Serve dusted with icing sugar. Store, well wrapped in the refrigerator, for up to 5 days.

400 g plain chocolate, roughly chopped

40 g cocoa powder

3 tablespoons strong espresso coffee

2 tablespoons brandy

6 large eggs, at room temperature

100 g golden caster sugar

250 ml double cream, chilled

icing sugar, for dusting

a loaf tin, 22 x 11 x 7 cm, greased and base-lined

a bain-marie or roasting tin

Serves 8

chocolate brûlée

This pudding is very rich, so serve
in small portions.

**600 ml thick single cream or thin
pouring double cream (avoid
extra-thick double cream)**

1 vanilla pod, split

**300 g plain chocolate,
finely chopped**

4 medium egg yolks

60 g icing sugar, sifted

**about 3 tablespoons caster
sugar, for sprinkling**

*8 ovenproof ramekins (or similar),
150 ml each*

a bain-marie or roasting tin

Serves 8

Put the cream and the split vanilla pod in a heavy saucepan. Heat
until scalding hot but not boiling. Remove the pan from the heat,
cover and let infuse for 15 minutes.

Lift out the vanilla pod and scrape the seeds into the cream with
the tip of a small knife.

Stir the chocolate into the cream until melted and smooth. Put the
egg yolks and icing sugar in a medium bowl, beat with a wooden
spoon until well blended, then stir in the warm chocolate cream.
When thoroughly mixed, pour into the ramekins.

Stand the dishes in a bain-marie (a roasting tin half-filled with
warm water) and bake in a preheated oven at 180°C (350°F) Gas 4
for about 30 minutes until just firm. Remove from the bain-marie
and let cool. Cover and chill overnight or for up to 48 hours.

Sprinkle a little sugar over the tops of the puddings, then put
under a preheated very hot grill for just a few minutes to
caramelize. A warning: if the ramekins are left for too long under
the grill, the chocolate cream will melt. Serve within 1 hour.

sweet
tarts & pies

pastry basics

A tart or pie should be a successful combination of a delicious filling and a melt-in-the-mouth pastry.

Pastry is most easily made in a food processor, so don't worry if you have hot hands or a less than light touch. Just follow the rules; don't overwork or overstretch the pastry, or it will be tough and heavy, and don't allow the fats to turn oily or start to melt as you work the dough, as this makes for soggy, greasy pastry. Use fats straight from the fridge, chill the dough before rolling out, then again before baking.

The pastry in most of these recipes is made in a food processor. However, to make pastry by hand, sift the dry ingredients into a bowl. Add very cold, diced fat and toss until it is lightly coated in flour. Cut the fat into smaller pieces using a round-bladed knife or a wire pastry cutter. Gently rub the fat and flour between your fingertips (not your palms) a little at a time until the mixture looks like fine crumbs with no large lumps. As you work, lift your hands up to the rim of the bowl to aerate the mixture as it falls back down.

Bind the mixture with iced water, egg yolk or other liquid using just enough to make a soft dough. If the dough is dry and hard, it will be difficult to use; if it is too wet and sticky, it will be tough and heavy when baked. As soon as the dough comes together turn it out on to a lightly floured surface and gently and briefly knead it to make it smooth and even.

To line a flan tin, roll out the pastry on a lightly floured surface to the diameter of the tin plus twice its height. Roll the dough around the rolling pin and lift it over the tin. Gently unroll the dough so it drapes over the tin. Carefully press the dough onto the bottom of the tin and up the sides so there are no pockets of air. Roll the pin over the top of the tin to cut off the excess dough. The sides of the pastry case should stand slightly above the rim. So use your thumbs to press the pastry sides upwards to make a neat rim about 5 mm higher than the tin. Curve your forefinger inside this rim and gently press the pastry over your finger so it curves inwards to make unmoulding easier.

Baking blind produces a crisp pastry case. Prick the pastry with a fork, cut a round of non-stick baking parchment the same size as the pastry lining the tin, crumple the paper to make it flexible, open out and gently press into the pastry case to cover the base and sides (easier if the pastry is chilled). Fill the lined case with ceramic baking beans, dried beans or uncooked rice to weigh it down. Bake in a preheated oven at 200°C (400°F) Gas 6 for 15 minutes until lightly golden and just firm. Carefully remove the paper and beans, then lower the temperature to 180°C (350°F) Gas 4. Bake for 5–7 minutes until crisp and lightly golden.

To bake a filled tart, set it on a hot baking sheet in the oven – the pastry will receive extra heat from the baking sheet, which will prevent it from becoming soggy.

FRUIT PIES

lemon meringue pie

175 g plain flour

a pinch of salt

20 g golden caster sugar

115 g unsalted butter, chilled and diced

1 large egg yolk mixed with 2 teaspoons iced water

Lemon Filling

freshly squeezed juice and grated zest of 3 medium unwaxed lemons

40 g cornflour

300 ml water

2 large egg yolks

85 g golden caster sugar

50 g unsalted butter, diced

Meringue Topping

3 large egg whites

140 g golden caster sugar

a loose-based flan tin, 21.5 cm diameter

Serves 6–8

To make the pastry in a food processor, put the flour, salt, sugar and butter in the bowl and process until the mixture resembles fine crumbs.

With the machine running, add the egg yolk and water through the feed tube. Process just until the dough comes together. If there are dry crumbs in the bottom of the bowl, add a little more water, 1 teaspoon at a time, until you have a slightly firm dough.

To make the pastry by hand, sift the flour, salt and sugar into a large bowl then rub in the diced butter using the tips of your fingers. When the mixture resembles breadcrumbs stir in the egg yolk and water mixture using a round-bladed knife – the mixture should not be dry and crumbly or soft and sticky.

In warm weather, wrap the dough and chill for 15 minutes until firm. Roll out on a lightly floured surface to a circle about 26 cm across and use to line the flan tin. Prick the bottom of the pastry case all over with a fork, then chill for about 15 minutes.

Bake the pastry case blind as described on page 71 in a preheated oven at 200°C (400°F) Gas 6 for 15 minutes until lightly golden and just firm.

Carefully remove the baking parchment and beans, lower the oven temperature to 180°C (350°F) Gas 4 and bake for a further 5–7 minutes or until the base is crisp and lightly golden.

Remove the pastry case from the oven and let cool while making the filling. Leave the oven at the same temperature.

Put the grated lemon zest and juice in a heatproof bowl. Add the cornflour and 1–2 tablespoons of the water and stir to make a smooth paste.

Bring the rest of the water to the boil in a medium saucepan, then stir into the lemon mixture. When thoroughly combined, tip the contents of the bowl back into the saucepan and cook, stirring constantly, until the mixture boils.

Reduce the heat and simmer, stirring frequently, for about 2 minutes until the mixture is smooth and thick.

Remove the pan from the heat and beat in the egg yolks and sugar, followed by the butter.

Spoon the filling into the pastry case and smooth the surface.

To make the topping, put the 3 egg whites in a non-plastic, spotlessly clean, grease-free bowl and whisk until soft peaks form. Whisk in the sugar, 1 tablespoon at a time, then whisk well to make a stiff, shiny meringue.

Gently spread the meringue over the lemon filling until it is completely covered.

Bake for 15–20 minutes in the preheated oven until the meringue is a good golden brown.

Remove from the oven, let cool, then unmould. Serve at room temperature within 24 hours of baking.

A traditional favourite recipe, with a delicious lemon filling made rich and creamy with the addition of butter.

cherry almond pie

250 g plain flour

a good pinch of salt

50 g ground almonds

85 g icing sugar

175 g unsalted butter, chilled and diced

1 large egg yolk mixed with 1 teaspoon iced water

caster sugar, for sprinkling

Cherry Filling

2 tablespoons slivered almonds

500 g large black cherries, stoned, or frozen cherries*

2 teaspoons cornflour

1–2 tablespoons light brown muscovado sugar, or to taste

a pie plate, 26 cm diameter

a baking sheet

Serves 6

*If using frozen cherries, use them straight from the freezer. Sprinkle the slivered almonds over the pastry base and increase the amount of cornflour to 1 tablespoon.

Put the flour, salt, almonds and icing sugar in a food processor and process. Add the butter and process until the mixture resembles fine crumbs. With the motor running, add the egg yolk and water through the feed tube and process just until the mixture comes together. If there are dry crumbs and the dough does not come together, add iced water a little at a time. Wrap the dough and chill for 15 minutes.

To prepare the filling, put a slivered almond into the cavity of each cherry. Mix with the cornflour and sugar.

Preheat the oven to 200°C (400°F) Gas 6 and put a baking sheet in to heat.

Divide the dough in two, one part slightly smaller than the other. Roll out the small piece on a lightly floured surface to a circle 29 cm across and use to line the pie plate, letting the excess drape over the rim. Spoon in the filling, leaving a border around the rim clear and mounding the fruit in the centre. Brush the pastry rim with cold water. Roll out the remaining pastry to a 29 cm circle. Roll it around the rolling pin, then unroll over the pie draping it over the filling. To seal, press the top crust firmly on to the dampened rim then, using a small knife, cut around the edge of the crust to cut off the excess dough. Crimp the rim with the back of a fork or your fingertips. Make a steam hole in the centre with a sharp knife and decorate the top with pastry leaves. Set the pie plate on the hot baking sheet and cook in the preheated oven for 20 minutes.

Reduce the temperature to 180°C (350°F) Gas 4 and bake for 10 minutes or until the pastry is golden. Sprinkle with sugar and serve warm or at room temperature within 24 hours of baking.

apricot crunch

Dried apricots, soaked in orange juice,
make this an easy store-cupboard fruit pie.

To make the filling, put the apricots, orange juice and cinnamon stick in a non-aluminium saucepan and bring to the boil. Remove the pan from the heat and let cool completely – preferably overnight. Drain thoroughly and discard the cinnamon stick.

To make the crust, put the flour, oats, sugar and ground cinnamon in a bowl and stir to mix. Add the diced butter and rub in with your fingertips until the mixture resembles very coarse crumbs. Add the beaten egg and briefly mix into the crumbs with your fingers to make pea-sized lumps of dough – do not overmix or bind the dough together.

Set aside a third of the mixture. Scatter the remainder into the pie dish and press on to the base and up the sides using the back of a spoon or a fork. Spoon in the drained filling then lightly scatter over the reserved crust mixture.

Bake in a preheated oven at 190°C (375°F) Gas 5 for about 30 minutes until crisp and golden. Serve warm or at room temperature with ice cream or fromage frais. Eat within 24 hours of baking.

150 g plain flour

60 g porridge oats

150 g light brown muscovado sugar

2 teaspoons ground cinnamon

175 g unsalted butter, chilled and dice

1 large egg, beaten

ice cream or fromage frais, to serve

Apricot Filling

250 g dried apricots

200 ml unsweetened orange juice

1 cinnamon stick

a round pie dish, 21.5 cm diameter and about 4 cm deep

Serves 4–6

Make this pie with your favourite berries. Mulberries were once rare, but are now available in season in good fruit shops and supermarkets.

apple and berry deep-dish pie

Put the flour, salt, sugar and butter in a food processor and process until the mixture looks like fine crumbs. With the machine running, gradually add the water through the feed tube to make a soft but not sticky dough. Wrap the dough and chill it.

Gently mix the apples with the berries and a little sugar to taste. If the apples are not juicy, add 1 tablespoon water or lemon juice. Spoon the fruit into the pie dish, heaping it up well in the middle to support the pastry.

Roll out the dough on a lightly floured work surface to an oval about 7.5 cm larger than your pie dish all the way around. Cut off a strip of dough about 1 cm wide, and long enough to go around the rim of the dish. Dampen the rim of the dish and paste on the strip of dough, joining the ends neatly. Dampen this pastry rim. Carefully cover the pie with the rest of the pastry, pressing it on to the rim to seal. With a sharp knife, trim the excess dough and use to decorate the top. Push up the sides of the crust with a small knife, then crimp or flute the pastry rim. Make a steam hole in the centre with a sharp knife.

Bake the pie in a preheated oven at 200°C (400°F) Gas 6 for about 30 minutes until the pastry is crisp and golden. Sprinkle with sugar and serve warm or at room temperature.

180 g plain flour

a good pinch of salt

1 teaspoon golden caster sugar

90 g unsalted butter, chilled and diced

about 4 tablespoons iced water, to bind

caster sugar, for sprinkling

Apple and Berry Filling

about 900 g Bramley apples or crisp tart eating apples, peeled, cored and thickly sliced

250 g raspberries, mulberries, loganberries or tayberries

2 tablespoons golden caster sugar, or to taste

1 tablespoon water or freshly squeezed lemon juice (optional)

a deep, oval pie dish, about 22 cm long

Serves 6

FRUIT TARTS

fresh raspberry criss-cross tart

230 g plain flour

½ teaspoon baking powder

60 g unblanched almonds

1 teaspoon ground cinnamon

100 g golden caster sugar

115 g unsalted butter, chilled and diced

1 medium egg, plus 1 egg yolk

sugar, for sprinkling

Raspberry Filling

250 g fresh raspberries*

1–2 teaspoons caster sugar, or to taste

1 rounded teaspoon cornflour

a loose-based flan tin, 21.5 cm diameter

a baking sheet

Serves 6

*Avoid washing the fruit if possible. Pick it over well, checking for blemishes and bugs.

To make the pastry, put the flour, baking powder, almonds, cinnamon and sugar in a food processor and process until the mixture resembles fine sand.

Add the pieces of chilled butter and process again until the mixture resembles fine crumbs. With the machine running, add the egg and yolk through the feed tube and process to make a soft dough. Wrap the dough and chill for at least 30 minutes until firm enough to roll out.

Turn out the dough on to a floured work surface and roll it out fairly thickly to a circle about 25 cm across. Use the pastry to line the flan tin, pressing the dough on to the base and sides. Trim off the excess pastry and use small pieces to repair any tears or holes, saving the remainder to make the strips of pastry lattice later. Chill the base and excess pastry.

Preheat the oven to 190°C (375°F) Gas 5 and put a baking sheet in to heat.

To make the filling, mix the fresh raspberries with the sugar and cornflour.

Re-roll the excess pastry and cut it into wide strips.

Spoon the filling into the pastry-lined flan tin and dampen the top edge of the pastry with water. Arrange the pastry strips in a lattice on top, pressing the ends onto the top edge to seal.

Set the flan case on the hot baking sheet and cook in the preheated oven until golden – about 25 minutes. Remove from the oven and sprinkle with sugar.

Serve warm or at room temperature within 2 days of baking.

VARIATIONS

Strawberry Liqueur Lattice Tart

To vary the fresh fruit filling, omit the raspberries and sugar and substitute the same quantity of the finest quality strawberry jam or strawberry compote, mixed with about 2 tablespoons schnapps or kirsch liqueur, to taste.

Proceed as in the main recipe. The alcohol will cut the sweetness of the jam filling.

Greengage, Apricot or Cherry Lattice Tart

For these three delicious variations, omit the raspberries and replace with a similar quantity of other fresh fruit. Choose from quartered, stoned fresh plums such as greengages or Victorias, halved and stoned fresh ripe apricots or stoned fresh ripe red cherries.

Sprinkle with 2 tablespoons liqueur such as slivovitz (plum brandy) or kirsch and proceed as in the main recipe.

A fresh fruit version of Linzertorte, the classic pastry from the town of Linz in Austria. The rich pastry is flavoured and coloured by almonds still in their brown papery skins, giving extra taste and texture.

blueberry cheesecake tart

150 g digestive biscuits, crushed

40 g golden caster sugar

70 g unsalted butter, melted

Lemon Cheese Filling

700 g cream cheese

1 teaspoon real vanilla essence

grated zest of 1 large unwaxed lemon

4 large eggs, beaten

150 g golden caster sugar

Blueberry Topping

grated zest of ½ large unwaxed lemon

450 ml soured cream

½ teaspoon real vanilla essence

1 tablespoon golden caster sugar

250 g fresh or frozen blueberries

a springform pan, 23 cm diameter, greased

a baking sheet

Serves 8–12

A combination of baked lemon cheesecake and blueberry pie – the topping is added towards the end of baking.

To make the crust, mix the biscuit crumbs with the sugar and butter. Tip into the prepared pan and press on to the base and halfway up the sides, using the back of a spoon. Chill the base while you make the filling.

Put the cream cheese (at room temperature), vanilla essence and lemon zest in an electric mixer or food processor and mix at low speed until very smooth. Gradually beat in the eggs, increasing the speed as the mixture becomes softer. When thoroughly mixed, beat in the sugar. Pour the filling into the biscuit crust and set the pan on a baking sheet. Bake in a preheated oven at 180°C (350°F) Gas 4 for 45 minutes. Remove the cheesecake from the oven and let cool a little – do not turn off the oven.

To make the topping, put the lemon zest, soured cream, vanilla essence and sugar in a bowl and mix well. Spread the mixture gently over the top of the cheesecake. Top with the blueberries, then bake for 10 minutes more.

Remove from the oven and let cool. Let chill overnight, then unmould. Remove from the refrigerator 30 minutes before serving. Store in a covered container in the refrigerator for up to 4 days.

To avoid a soggy pastry base, cook it thoroughly first, brush with egg white to seal, then cook the filled tart on a preheated baking sheet.

lemon tart

150 g plain flour

a pinch of salt

85 g unsalted butter, chilled and diced

25 g golden caster sugar

1 large egg yolk

1–2 tablespoons iced water

a little egg white, lightly beaten, for brushing

Lemon Filling

3 large eggs, plus 1 egg yolk

150 ml double cream

100 g golden caster sugar

grated zest of 2 large unwaxed lemons

freshly squeezed juice of 3 large lemons

a loose-based flan tin, 23 cm diameter

a baking sheet

Serves 6

To make the pastry, put the flour, salt, butter and sugar in a food processor and process until the mixture resembles fine sand. With the machine running, add the egg yolk and water through the feed tube and process just until the dough comes together. Wrap the dough and chill for about 30 minutes.

Roll out the dough on a lightly floured work surface to a circle about 28 cm across. Use to line the flan tin. Prick the base of the pastry case with a fork, then chill for 15 minutes.

Bake the pastry case blind as described on page 71 in a preheated oven at 190°C (375°F) Gas 5, then remove from the oven. Do not unmould but immediately brush the base with a little egg white, then let cool. Reduce the oven temperature to 170°C (325°F) Gas 3 and put a baking sheet in the oven to heat.

To make the filling, put all the ingredients in a large jug and beat by hand until just combined. Set the pastry case, in the flan tin, on the hot baking sheet and pour in three-quarters of the filling. Put the tart in the oven, then carefully pour in the remaining filling (this way you avoid spilling the filling as you put the tart into the oven).

Bake for 25–30 minutes or until the filling is firm when the tart is gently shaken. Remove from the oven and let cool before unmoulding. Serve at room temperature or chilled within 2 days.

apple and treacle tart

To make the pastry, put the flour, salt and butter in a food processor and process until the mixture resembles fine crumbs. With the machine running add 2 tablespoons iced water through the feed tube – the mixture should come together to make a firm dough. If the dough does not form a ball and is stiff and crumbly, add a little more water. In warm weather, or if the dough seems soft, wrap and chill for about 20 minutes.

Roll out the dough on a lightly floured work surface to a large circle about 28 cm across and use to line the pie dish. Press the pastry on to the base of the dish to eliminate any pockets of air, then trim off the excess pastry with a sharp knife. The pastry scraps can be saved for decorations. Decorate the rim of the tart by pressing the pastry with the prongs of a fork. Chill the pastry base while making the filling.

Peel, core and coarsely grate the apple, then mix with the golden syrup, breadcrumbs, lemon zest and juice. Spoon the mixture on to the pastry base – don't press down to level the surface or compress the filling as you will lose its fluffy texture.

You can decorate the tart with pastry scraps cut into leaves or apple shapes, if you like. Bake in a preheated oven at 190°C (375°F) Gas 5 for about 30 minutes until golden. Serve warm or at room temperature within 48 hours of baking.

Bramley cooking apples turn light and fluffy when cooked.

220 g plain flour

a good pinch of salt

160 g unsalted butter, chilled and diced

2–3 tablespoons iced water, to bind

Apple Treacle Filling

1 large cooking apple

3 rounded tablespoons golden syrup

25 g fresh white breadcrumbs

grated zest and freshly squeezed juice of 1 large unwaxed lemon

a pie dish, 26 cm diameter

Serves 6–8

fig tart

This is a summery tart that makes a spectacular dinner-party dish. Crisp puff pastry is topped with ripe figs and orange-flavoured pastry cream.

Roll out the pastry on a lightly floured work surface to a circle 32 cm across. Use to line the flan tin, letting the excess drape over the rim. Chill the pastry for about 15 minutes, then cut off the excess dough with a sharp knife.

Prick the base of the pastry with a fork, then line the flan case with parchment paper, fill with baking beans and bake blind (see page 71) in a preheated oven at 200°C (400°F) Gas 6 for 12–15 minutes until set.

Remove the beans and paper, then bake for about 10 minutes more until crisp and cooked through. Remove from the oven and let cool while you prepare the fruit and filling.

Sprinkle the figs with the liqueur and leave to macerate for 2 hours or overnight.

To make the pastry cream, put the milk in a saucepan and heat almost to boiling point. Put the egg yolks and sugar in a bowl and whisk until light and thick, then whisk in the flour. When the mixture is smooth, beat in the milk. Tip the mixture back into the saucepan and cook, stirring constantly, until it boils and thickens. Simmer gently, still stirring, for 2 minutes, then remove from the heat. Sprinkle with a little sugar to prevent a skin forming and let cool.

When you are ready to serve, fold the whipped cream and liqueur into the pastry cream and spoon it into the pastry case. Drain the figs and reserve the liqueur. Arrange the fruit on top of the pastry cream filling. Heat the apricot jelly or jam until smooth and very hot, then stir in the liqueur and quickly brush over the figs. Serve immediately.

300 g ready-made puff pastry

Fig Topping

12 ripe figs, rinsed, trimmed and halved (or cut in quarters if very large)

3 tablespoons Grand Marnier, Cointreau or other orange liqueur

4 tablespoons apricot jelly or sieved jam, to finish

Pastry Cream Filling

300 ml whole milk

4 large egg yolks

55 g golden caster sugar

2 tablespoons plain flour

140 ml double cream, whipped

2 tablespoons Grand Marnier, Cointreau or other orange liqueur

sugar, for sprinkling

a loose-based flan tin, 25 cm diameter

Serves 8

apple cinnamon tart

To make the pastry, put the flour, salt and sugar in a food processor and process just until combined.

Add the butter and process until the mixture resembles fine crumbs. With the machine running, add the egg yolk and water through the feed tube and process just until the mixture comes together to make a slightly firm dough. If there are dry crumbs add a little extra water, 1 teaspoon at a time. Wrap the dough and chill it for about 20 minutes.

Meanwhile preheat the oven to 200°C (400°F) Gas 6 and put a baking sheet in the oven to heat up.

Roll out the pastry on a lightly floured work surface to a large circle about 29 cm across. Use to line the flan case, then chill while preparing the filling.

Peel, quarter and core the apples, then grate coarsely. Add the cinnamon, sugar and dried fruit and mix well. Pile into the flan case. Spoon over the golden syrup, then dot with the pieces of butter. Set the flan tin on the hot baking sheet and cook in the preheated oven for about 20 minutes.

Remove from the oven and let cool for 1 minute, then unmould. Serve warm. Eat within 2 days of baking.

A good recipe to make with windfall apples, and a change from the usual sliced apple pies.

180 g plain flour

a pinch of salt

20 g golden caster sugar

120 g unsalted butter, chilled and diced

1 egg yolk mixed with 3 teaspoons iced water

Apple Cinnamon Filling

3 large Bramley apples, about 1 kg total weight

2 teaspoons ground cinnamon

60 g golden caster sugar, or to taste

30 g raisins, dried cherries or dried cranberries

2 tablespoons golden syrup

30 g unsalted butter, chilled and diced

a loose-based flan tin, 23 cm diameter

a baking sheet

Serves 6

caramelized pear tart

200 g plain flour

a pinch of salt

30 g ground almonds

30 g caster sugar

100 g unsalted butter, chilled and diced

1 egg yolk

2–3 tablespoons iced water

Caramelized Pear Filling

115 g unsalted butter, thinly sliced

200 g golden caster sugar

whole blanched almonds

about 2 kg Williams or Comice pears, slightly under-ripe, peeled, halved and cored

a tarte tatin tin, or a frying pan with an ovenproof handle, 30.5 cm diameter

Serves 10

To make the pastry, put the flour, salt, ground almonds and sugar in a food processor and process briefly. Add the butter and process just until the mixture resembles fine crumbs. With the machine running, add the egg yolk and 2 tablespoons iced water through the feed tube. Process just until the mixture binds to make a fairly firm dough. If there are dry crumbs add a little extra water, 1 teaspoon at a time. Wrap the dough and chill it for 20 minutes.

To make the filling, arrange the sliced butter on the base of the tin or pan to cover the base completely. Sprinkle over an even layer of sugar, then almonds. Pack the pears into the pan, cut side down, then place over moderate heat on top of the stove and cook for 20 minutes or until the butter and sugar have formed a richly golden caramel.

Roll out the dough on a lightly floured work surface to a circle to fit the top of the tin or pan. Roll the dough around the rolling pin. Remove the pan from the heat and let cool for 1 minute to allow the bubbling to subside. Lift the rolling pin over the pan and gently unroll the dough so it covers the filling. Quickly tuck the edges inside the pan. Prick the pastry with a fork, then bake in a preheated oven at 220°C (425°F) Gas 7 for 20 minutes or until crisp and golden.

Remove the tart from the oven, leave for 5 minutes, then run a round-bladed knife around the edge to loosen the pastry. Place a large plate upside down over the top of the pan and invert the tart so the fruit is uppermost. Serve warm or at room temperature within 24 hours of baking.

flat plum tart

A German-style yeast-base tart.

To make the crust, put the flour, salt and sugar in a bowl and make a well in the centre. Crumble the yeast into a small bowl, add the milk and stir until smooth. Pour the liquid into the well in the flour. Add the egg and butter and gradually work in the flour to make a soft dough. Knead for 10 minutes until smooth and satiny – if the dough sticks to your fingers, work in extra flour 1 tablespoon at a time. The dough can be kneaded for 5 minutes using an electric mixer fitted with a dough hook, but do not use a food processor.

Cover the dough with a damp tea towel and let rise for 1 hour at room temperature.

To prepare the filling, toss the prepared plums with sugar, to taste and set aside.

To make the crumble topping, put the flour and sugar in a bowl and mix. Add the diced butter and rub in with your fingertips to make pea-sized clumps of dough. Stir in the nuts and set aside.

Knock down the risen dough with your knuckles, and roll or press it out to a rectangle about 32 x 24 cm. Transfer to the baking sheet and press back to the correct size. Top with the plums, cut side up, then sprinkle with the crumble topping.

Bake in a preheated oven at 190°C (375°F) Gas 5 for about 30 minutes until the base is golden, the fruit is tender and the topping is crisp and brown. Serve warm with cream within 24 hours of baking.

about 350 g strong white bread flour

½ teaspoon salt

50 g golden caster sugar

10 g fresh yeast

200 ml milk, lukewarm

1 medium egg, beaten

20 g unsalted butter, very soft

single cream, to serve

Plum Filling

500 g plums, halved and stoned

3 tablespoons demerara sugar

Crumble Topping

140 g plain flour

100 g light brown muscovado sugar

110 g unsalted butter, diced

200 g walnut or pecan pieces

a large baking sheet, greased

Serves 8

NUT TARTS & PIES

hazelnut strawberry tart

50 g hazelnuts

200 g plain flour

a pinch of salt

70 g icing sugar

175 g unsalted butter, chilled and diced

2 large egg yolks

ice cream, to serve (optional)

Strawberry Topping

500 g strawberries, raspberries, blueberries or a combination, plus extra to serve (optional)

225 g seedless raspberry jelly

1–2 tablespoons water

a large baking sheet, greased

Serves 8

Toast the hazelnuts in a preheated oven at 180°C (350°F) Gas 4 until they are a good golden brown – about 8 minutes. If necessary, remove the papery brown husks by rubbing the nuts together in a clean tea towel. Let cool.

Save about a dozen nuts for decoration. Put the rest in a food processor, add the flour and salt and process until the mixture resembles fine sand. Add the icing sugar and process briefly to mix. Add the diced butter and process until the mixture resembles breadcrumbs. With the machine running, add the egg yolks through the feed tube – process just until the mixture comes together. Wrap and chill until firm enough to roll out – about 30 minutes.

Roll or press out the dough on the greased baking sheet into a circle about 26 cm across. Flute the pastry (decorate the edges by pinching the dough between your fingers). Prick the base all over with a fork, then chill until firm – about 15 minutes.

If necessary, reheat the oven to 180°C (350°F) Gas 4. Bake the pastry base for about 20 minutes or until firm and light gold (beware – overcooked pastry will taste bitter).

Remove from the oven and let cool until quite firm, then transfer to a serving platter. Decorate the top with the reserved nuts and the strawberries – halved, or quartered if large – or other fruit.

Put the jelly and 1 tablespoon water in a small saucepan and heat. Beat until smooth. Bring to the boil, then brush over the fruit and nuts, completely covering them. Let set.

Serve with ice cream, if using. Eat within 2 days of baking.

VARIATIONS

Almond Strawberry Tart

Replace the hazelnuts with an equal quantity of blanched whole almonds. First toast the nuts in the oven until golden (take care not to let them burn), then cool. Save a few for decoration, then process the remainder with the flour and salt and proceed as in the main recipe.

Walnut Berry Tart

Omit the hazelnuts and substitute a similar quantity of walnut pieces – there is no need to toast them in the oven first. Proceed as in the main recipe.

Individual Strawberry Tarts

To make small, individual tarts to serve with tea or coffee, rather than as a pudding, cut the pastry into circles about 10 cm in diameter, using a biscuit cutter or a small saucer to cut around. Proceed as in the main recipe, baking at the same temperature for about 10–12 minutes.

A rich hazelnut biscuit base is covered with small berries – strawberries, raspberries, even blueberries will do – then glazed. Simple but glamorous.

pecan fudge pie

Really fresh pecan nuts are essential for this recipe.

To make the pastry, put the flour, salt and butter in a food processor and process until the mixture resembles fine crumbs. With the machine running, add 2 tablespoons water through the feed tube and process just until the dough comes together. If there are dry crumbs and the dough seems stiff add extra water, 1 teaspoon at a time, to make a fairly firm dough.

In warm weather it may be necessary to wrap and chill the dough for 20 minutes before rolling out.

To make the pastry by hand, sift the flour and salt into a large bowl then rub in the diced butter using the tips of your fingers. When the mixture resembles breadcrumbs stir in enough water to bring the pastry together to make a fairly firm dough.

Roll out the pastry on a lightly floured work surface to a circle about 26 cm across. Use to line the flan tin or pie dish, then chill.

To make the filling, let the butter cool to lukewarm. Put the eggs, sugar and vanilla essence in a bowl and beat lightly until frothy, then stir in the melted butter. Sift the flour with the salt and cocoa into the bowl, then fold in using a large metal spoon. When thoroughly mixed, stir in the pecans, then spoon into the pastry case. Bake in a preheated oven at 180°C (350°F) Gas 4 for about 25 minutes until just firm. Remove from the oven and let cool, then serve at room temperature. Eat within 3 days of baking.

170 g plain flour

a pinch of salt

90 g unsalted butter, chilled and diced

2–3 tablespoons iced water, to bind

Pecan Filling

115 g unsalted butter, melted

2 large eggs, beaten

175 g light brown muscovado sugar

1 teaspoon real vanilla essence

35 g plain flour

a good pinch of salt

30 g cocoa powder

150 g pecan halves

a loose-based flan tin or pie dish, 22 cm diameter

Serves 8

sticky walnut tart

175 g plain flour

a good pinch of salt

20 g golden caster sugar

100 g unsalted butter,
chilled and diced

1 egg yolk mixed with
2 teaspoons water

vanilla ice cream or crème
fraîche, to serve

Walnut Filling

175 g walnut halves

85 g unsalted butter

50 g golden caster sugar

50 g set honey

150 ml double cream

*a loose-based flan tin,
22 cm diameter*

Serves 8

To make the pastry, put the flour, salt, sugar and butter in a food processor and process until the mixture resembles fine crumbs. With the machine running add the egg yolk and water through the feed tube and process just until the mixture comes together. Wrap and chill the dough until firm – about 20 minutes.

Turn out the dough on to a lightly floured work surface and knead for a couple of seconds until smooth.

Roll out to a circle about 27 cm across, then use to line the flan tin. Roll the dough around the rolling pin and lift it over the flan tin. Gently unroll the dough so it drapes over the tin. Carefully press the dough on to the base of the tin and up the sides so there are no pockets of air. Roll the pin over the top of the tin to cut off the excess dough, then neaten the rim with your fingers. Chill for 15 minutes until firm.

Bake the pastry case blind as described on page 71 in a preheated oven at 190°C (375°F) Gas 5. Remove the paper and beans and bake for another 5 minutes to cook the base – it should be firm and just coloured.

Remove from the oven and let cool, but don't turn the oven off.

To make the filling, put the walnuts, butter, sugar and honey in a heavy frying pan, preferably non-stick. Cook, stirring, over low heat until the mixture is a pale straw gold. Stir in the cream and cook for 1 minute until bubbling.

Pour the walnut filling into the pastry case and bake for about 12 minutes until deep golden brown. Remove the tart from the oven, let cool, then unmould. Serve at room temperature with vanilla ice cream or crème fraîche. Eat within 2 days of baking.

pine nut honey tart

Always use fresh nuts and store opened packets in the freezer.

To make the pastry, put the flour, salt, butter and sugar in a food processor and process until the mixture resembles fine crumbs. With the motor running add the egg yolk and 1 tablespoon water through the feed tube and process until the dough just comes together. If there are dry crumbs or the dough is stiff, add extra water, 1 teaspoon at a time, to make a fairly firm dough. Wrap the dough and chill it for 20 minutes.

Roll out the dough on a lightly floured work surface to a circle about 28 cm across. Use to line the flan tin and chill while preparing the filling.

Heat the oven to 190°C (375°F) Gas 5 and put a baking sheet in the oven to heat.

To make the filling, put the butter in a bowl and beat until creamy using a wooden spoon or an electric mixer, then beat in the sugar and honey until light and fluffy. Gradually beat in the eggs, 1 tablespoon at a time. Stir in the ground almonds, then sift the flour, salt and baking powder into the bowl and mix gently using a large metal spoon.

Spoon into the pastry case and smooth the surface. Set the flan tin on the hot baking sheet and bake for 10 minutes. Gently remove from the oven and scatter the pine nuts on top of the filling. Bake for another 15 minutes until golden and just firm. Remove from the oven and let cool for 1 minute. Carefully unmould, let cool to room temperature, then serve. Eat within 2 days of baking.

150 g plain flour

a pinch of salt

90 g unsalted butter, chilled and diced

30 g golden caster sugar

1 large egg yolk

1–2 tablespoons iced water

Pine Nut Filling

55 g unsalted butter, at room temperature

75 g golden caster sugar

1 tablespoon honey

2 medium eggs, beaten

65 g ground almonds

20 g plain flour

a pinch of salt

½ teaspoon baking powder

100 g pine nuts

a loose-based flan tin, 22 cm diameter

Serves 6

pear and almond cream pie

Put the flour, salt and butter in a food processor and process until the mixture looks like fine crumbs. With the machine running slowly pour in the water through the feed tube – it should quickly come together to form a soft but not sticky dough. If there are dry crumbs work in extra water, 1 teaspoon at a time.

In warm weather it may be necessary to chill the dough until firm before rolling out. If so, wrap and chill the dough for 20 minutes. Turn out the dough on to a lightly floured work surface. Cut off one-third to make the base. Wrap and chill the rest.

Roll out the base to a circle 30 cm across and use to line the pie plate, pressing the pastry on to the base and rim to push out any air bubbles. Do not trim off the excess.

To make the filling, put the butter and marzipan in a food processor and process until smooth. Add the flour and eggs and process until very smooth. Spoon on to the pastry base leaving a border around the rim clear. Cut the pear quarters into 2–3 vertical slices, 1 cm thick. Put on top of the almond mixture, mounding the fruit in the centre.

To make the lid, roll out the reserved pastry to a circle about 31 cm across. Dampen the rim of the pie base, then cover with the pastry lid. Press the edges together firmly to seal. With a sharp knife cut off the excess pastry and cut three steam holes in the pastry lid.

Bake in a preheated oven at 190°C (375°F) Gas 5 for about 45 minutes or until golden brown. Remove from the oven, sprinkle with a little golden caster sugar and let cool. Serve warm or at room temperature and eat within 2 days of baking.

250 g plain flour

a pinch of salt

125 g unsalted butter, chilled and diced

3 tablespoons iced water, to bind

golden caster sugar, for sprinkling

Pear and Almond Cream

110 g unsalted butter, at room temperature

225 g white marzipan (almond paste), broken into pea-sized pieces

2 tablespoons plain flour

2 medium eggs, beaten

4 large slightly under-ripe pears, peeled, quartered and cored

a metal deep pie plate, 26 cm diameter

Serves 8

FRENCH & ITALIAN FLAVOURS

red fruit croustade

about 250 g filo pastry

about 120 g unsalted butter

golden caster sugar,
for sprinkling

icing sugar, for sprinkling

Red Fruit Filling

30 g unsalted butter

60 g fresh breadcrumbs

½ teaspoon ground
cinnamon (optional)

3–4 tablespoons golden caster
sugar, to taste

500 g mixed red fruit
(blackberries, raspberries,
redcurrants, blackcurrants,
cherries or strawberries)

1 teaspoon cornflour

*a springform pan,
30.5 cm diameter, well greased
and sprinkled with sugar*

Serves 8

If necessary, thaw the pastry according to the packet instructions. Once unwrapped, the pastry should be covered with a damp tea towel to keep it from drying out. If it becomes dry and hard, it will crack and become difficult to use. Meanwhile, melt the butter and leave to cool while preparing the filling.

To make the red fruit filling, first heat the butter in a small saucepan, then add the breadcrumbs and fry, stirring constantly, until golden brown.

Remove the pan from the heat and stir in the cinnamon, if using, and 1 tablespoon sugar. Let cool.

Gently toss the prepared fruit with the cornflour and the rest of the sugar, to taste.

Line the base of the prepared tin with 2–3 sheets of filo pastry, overlapping where necessary. Let the edges flop over the rim. Brush the sheets with the melted butter and sprinkle with a little caster sugar. Add another 2–3 sheets of pastry, brushing and sprinkling as before. Repeat once more (about half the pastry should have been used).

Spread the breadcrumb mixture evenly in the pastry case. Add the fruit filling but do not press it down.

Fold the edges of the filo over the filling as if wrapping a parcel. Brush the top with melted butter and sprinkle with caster sugar.

Lightly brush the remaining sheets of pastry with the melted butter, then cut or tear them in half. Crumple each piece of pastry like a chiffon scarf and gently arrange them in a pile on top of the pie. Sprinkle with any remaining

sugar and bake the croustade in a preheated oven at 220°C
(425°F) Gas 7 for 15–20 minutes until golden.

Remove the croustade from the oven. Carefully unclip the pan,
dust with icing sugar and serve. Eat within 24 hours.

VARIATIONS

Caramelized Apple Croustade

Replace the red fruit with 1 kg Bramley cooking apples, peeled and
thickly sliced. Heat 60 g butter in a saucepan and fry the apples
until golden. Sprinkle with 60 g golden caster sugar and cook until
the apples caramelize. Let cool, then proceed as in the main recipe.

Pineapple Croustade

Replace the red fruit with 1 medium
pineapple, peeled, cored and cut into
chunks. Heat 60 g butter in a saucepan
and fry the pieces of pineapple until
caramelized. Remove the pan from
the heat and stir in 2 tablespoons
rum. Let cool, then proceed as
in the main recipe.

Brands of filo pastry
vary tremendously –
I use Antoniou,
which is excellent,
others can be tough
and heavy. Ask other
cooks for the best
local product.

mango tartes tatin

Roll out the pastry on a lightly floured work surface as thinly as possible. Using a biscuit cutter or a saucer as a guide, cut out 6 rounds 11 cm across. Transfer to the baking sheets, prick well with a fork and chill while preparing the topping.

Peel the mangoes and cut the flesh away from the stones. Cut the flesh into strips about 1.5 cm thick. Chop the ginger very finely.

Put the butter in a heavy frying pan and heat, then add the ginger. Roll the mango slices in sugar, then fry in the hot butter until golden. Remove the mango to a plate and let cool.

Arrange the mango slices on the pastry rounds, then bake for 10–12 minutes in a preheated oven at 220°C (425°F) Gas 7 until the pastry is golden.

Decorate with the pistachio nuts and serve immediately. Eat within 24 hours.

Slices of mango are quickly browned in butter and sugar, flavoured with ginger and baked with puff pastry.

300 g ready-made puff pastry

3 slightly under-ripe mangoes

2 pieces stem ginger

90 g unsalted butter

70 g golden caster sugar

1 tablespoon shelled pistachio nuts, blanched

2 large baking sheets

Serves 6

crème brûlée tart

180 g plain flour

a good pinch of salt

30 g golden caster sugar

90 g unsalted butter, chilled and diced

1 large egg yolk mixed with 1 teaspoon water

55 g granulated sugar, for sprinkling

Raspberry Filling

115 g fresh raspberries

4 large egg yolks

60 g golden caster sugar

400 ml double cream

1 vanilla pod, split

55 g unsalted butter, diced, at room temperature

a deep, loose-based flan tin, 23 cm diameter

Serves 8

To make the pastry, put the flour, salt and sugar in a food processor and process until just mixed. Add the butter and process until the mixture resembles fine crumbs. With the machine running, add the egg yolk and water through the feed tube and process just until the dough comes together. Wrap and chill the dough for 30 minutes.

Roll out the dough on a lightly floured work surface to a circle about 29 cm across and use to line the flan tin. Chill for 10–15 minutes.

Prick the pastry base with a fork, then cover with a circle of greaseproof paper, fill it with baking beans and bake blind in a preheated oven at 200°C (400°F) Gas 6 for 10 minutes. Remove the beans and paper and bake for 15 minutes more until the base is crisp and golden. Remove from the oven and let cool, but do not unmould.

To make the filling, first arrange the raspberries in the base of the cooked flan case. Put the egg yolks and sugar in a heatproof bowl and whisk until very thick and frothy.

Put the cream and vanilla pod in a saucepan and heat until steaming hot, but not boiling. Pour the cream on to the egg mixture in a slow, steady stream, whisking constantly. Put the bowl over a saucepan of steaming, not boiling, water and cook slowly, stirring constantly, until thick – about 10 minutes. Remove the bowl from the heat and take out the vanilla pod. Gradually whisk in the butter, then pour the mixture into the pastry case. Let cool, then chill for several hours or overnight until firm and set.

Sprinkle the tart with granulated sugar, then brown under a preheated hot grill for a few minutes. Let cool, then chill for 2–3 hours before serving. Eat within 24 hours.

torta di ricotta with chocolate pieces

160 g plain flour

20 g cocoa powder

a good pinch of salt

60 g icing sugar

110 g unsalted butter, chilled and diced

Ricotta Filling

250 g ricotta cheese

40 g icing sugar

the grated zest of 1 unwaxed orange

1 teaspoon orange liqueur or real vanilla essence

1 large egg, plus 1 yolk

100 g plain chocolate, coarsely chopped

30 g flaked almonds, for sprinkling

a loose-based flan tin, 22 cm diameter

Serves 8

The case is made from a rich chocolate biscuit mixture, and the light filling is ricotta studded with chunks of bitter chocolate.

To make the pastry, put the flour, cocoa, salt and icing sugar in a food processor and process briefly just to mix. Add the pieces of butter and process until the mixture resembles fine sand, then pulse the machine until the dough comes together. Wrap and chill the dough for 20 minutes.

Roll out the dough on a lightly floured work surface to a circle about 27 cm across and use to line the flan tin. The pastry is quite hard to work so mend any holes that appear with trimmings and press the dough together, if necessary. Chill the pastry case while preparing the filling.

To make the filling, put the ricotta in a bowl and beat until creamy using a wooden spoon. Beat in the icing sugar, followed by the orange zest and liqueur or vanilla essence. When completely mixed, beat in the egg and the egg yolk, then stir in the chocolate. Spoon the mixture into the pastry case and sprinkle with the almonds.

Bake the tart in a preheated oven at 180°C (350°F) Gas 4 for about 25 minutes until firm.

Remove from the oven and let cool, then unmould. Serve at room temperature. Eat within 2 days.

torta di zabaglione

Marsala wine is traditionally used to make zabaglione, but if you find it too sweet in this dish, substitute dry white wine instead.

Toast the almonds in a preheated oven at 180°C (350°F) Gas 4 for 10–12 minutes until light golden. Let cool. Reduce the oven temperature to 150°C (300°F) Gas 2.

To make the base, put the almonds and icing sugar in a food processor and process until the mixture resembles fine sand.

Put the egg whites in a spotlessly clean, grease-free, non-plastic bowl. Beat with a wire whisk or electric mixer until stiff peaks form, then beat in the caster sugar, 1 tablespoon at a time. Using a large metal spoon, gently fold in the almond mixture and liqueur or almond essence. Spoon the mixture into the piping bag and pipe a flat coil to cover the base of the prepared pan. Pipe a rim inside the edge of the pan.

Bake the base for about 30 minutes until quite hard and golden brown. Remove from the oven and let cool, then unclip the pan and peel off the paper. Put the base on a platter and set aside.

To make the filling, put the egg yolks, sugar and wine or Marsala in a heatproof bowl set over a saucepan of boiling water. Whisk until the mixture is thick and foamy. Remove the bowl from the heat and whisk until cool. When completely cold, fold in the whipped cream, then spoon the mixture on to the base.

Sprinkle with fresh fruit and serve at once.

225 g whole blanched almonds

1 tablespoon icing sugar

2 large egg whites

80 g golden caster sugar

1 teaspoon Amaretto liqueur or ½ teaspoon real almond essence

fresh fruit, to finish

Zabaglione Filling

4 large egg yolks*

3 tablespoons golden caster sugar

100 ml dry white wine or Marsala

150 ml double cream, chilled and whipped

a springform pan, 23 cm diameter, greased and lined

a large piping bag, fitted with a 1 cm plain tube

Serves 6

*See note regarding uncooked eggs, page 4.

cookies, biscuits & biscotti

a little indulgence

A homemade biscuit is a small luxury. It turns a coffee break or a midnight snack into a moment of sheer pleasure – a little self-indulgence to warm your own day, or hospitality to brighten someone else's. Making biscuits is easy, but a few pointers may be helpful.

Most importantly, you need good ingredients for good results. I always use unrefined, pure cane sugars (except refined icing sugar for decoration), because they have a slightly deeper flavour.

I prefer unsalted butter: the taste is better and the cook controls how much salt is used in the recipe.

I also prefer medium or large free-range eggs and use them at room temperature. They taste better and produce better results than battery-farmed eggs.

Organic and stoneground flours are sold in most supermarkets – I use them because they are healthier and have better flavour.

Nuts should be as fresh as possible: the oils they contain quickly turn rancid when exposed to air, so always store open packets in the freezer.

Use plain chocolate with at least 70 per cent cocoa solids: supermarket own-labels are usually of very good quality and value. When white chocolate is called for – use best quality, not children's white bars.

When using lemon or orange zest, use unwaxed fruit and wash the fruit well before removing the zest.

Best quality real vanilla essence should always be used. Because vanilla is expensive, some of the essence available is either low-grade or fake and chemical and therefore smells and tastes very harsh.

It is worth investing in good tools – they make baking easier and more successful. Accurate scales and measuring spoons are essential (see page 4 for spoon measurements). Electric mixers and food processors don't just save time, they also make complicated recipes easier, less messy and less exhausting.

Biscuits scorch easily, so thin, cheap baking sheets can ruin the best recipe and the most careful preparation. Heavy, professional-quality sheets or those specially made for biscuits are wise investments and last forever.

Good airtight containers are vital for storage – biscuits soon lose their crispness in humid conditions.

An oven thermometer is also very useful. Each oven is an individual – most are temperamental. Learn how yours behaves, how quickly it warms up, how well it retains heat and where the hot spots are.

Baking times in these recipes are only guidelines, so know your oven and watch your biscuits carefully.

TRADITIONAL BISCUITS

wheaten biscuits

Two versions of a classic biscuit.

170 g stoneground wholemeal flour

a good pinch of salt

1 teaspoon baking powder

50 g porridge oats

40 g golden granulated sugar

100 g unsalted butter, chilled and diced

a round biscuit or scone cutter, 7.5 cm diameter

several baking sheets, greased

Makes about 16

Put all the ingredients in a food processor and process until the dough comes together. (In very cold weather, you may have to work the lumps of dough together with your hands.)

Roll out the dough on a lightly floured work surface to about 5 mm thick. Using a 7.5 cm round biscuit or scone cutter, cut the dough into rounds. Knead the trimmings together, re-roll, then cut out more rounds.

Arrange the biscuits on the prepared baking sheets and prick them well with a fork. Bake in a preheated oven at 190°C (375°F) Gas 5 for 12–15 minutes until they turn colour slightly at the edges.

Remove from the oven and let cool on the baking sheets for 3–4 minutes until firm enough to transfer to a wire rack. Let cool completely, then store in an airtight container. Best eaten within 1 week, or freeze for up to 1 month.

VARIATION

Savoury Wheaten Biscuits

reduce the granulated sugar in the main recipe to 20 g

add ¼ teaspoon curry powder or garam masala, or 1 teaspoon ground cinnamon or ginger

Makes about 16

Make the dough as in the main recipe, reducing the quantity of sugar and adding the spices. Proceed as in the main recipe and serve with cheese.

oat and raisin biscuits

Make these biscuits with dried sour cherries or dried cranberries instead of raisins for an unusual and flavourful alternative.

Put the flour, salt, baking powder and oats in a bowl and mix.

Put the butter, sugar and vanilla essence in a separate bowl and cream until fluffy using a wooden spoon or electric mixer.

Using your hands or a wooden spoon, gradually work the flour mixture and dried fruit into the creamed butter, then knead the mixture until it comes together. Divide the dough into about 32 equal pieces and roll them into balls about 3 cm across.

Place the balls well apart on the baking sheets, then flatten them slightly with your fingers.

Cook in a preheated oven at 180°C (350°F) Gas 4 for 10–12 minutes or until golden.

Remove from the oven and let cool on the baking sheet for a couple of minutes until firm enough to transfer to a wire rack. Let cool completely, then store in an airtight container. Best eaten within 1 week, or freeze for up to 1 month.

250 g self-raising flour

a pinch of salt

1 teaspoon baking powder

175 g porridge oats

250 g unsalted butter, at room temperature

200 g golden caster sugar

½ teaspoon real vanilla essence

50 g raisins, dried sour cherries or dried cranberries

several baking sheets, greased

Makes about 32

old-fashioned gingernuts

350 g self-raising flour

a pinch of salt

200 g golden caster sugar

1 tablespoon ground ginger

1 teaspoon bicarbonate of soda

115 g unsalted butter

85 g golden syrup

1 large egg, beaten

several baking sheets, greased

Makes 30

Sift the flour into a mixing bowl with the salt, sugar, ginger and bicarbonate of soda. Put the butter and golden syrup in a small saucepan and heat very gently, stirring occasionally, until the butter melts. Remove the pan from the heat, let cool until just warm, then pour on to the dry ingredients. Add the egg and mix thoroughly.

Using your hands, roll the dough into 30 walnut-sized balls. Place the balls well apart on the prepared baking sheets, then flatten slightly with your fingers.

Cook in a preheated oven at 170°C (325°F) Gas 3 for 15–20 minutes or until golden brown. Remove from the oven and leave on the sheets for 1 minute to firm up, then transfer to a wire rack to cool completely.

Store in an airtight container and eat within 1 week, or freeze for up to 1 month.

If you like gingernuts chewy, cook them for about 15 minutes until just firm. If you prefer them crunchy, cook just a few minutes longer.

A traditional biscuit from the
West Country.

cornish fairings

100 g plain flour
a pinch of salt
1 teaspoon baking powder
½ teaspoon bicarbonate of soda
1 teaspoon ground ginger
½ teaspoon ground mixed spice
40 g golden caster sugar
**50 g unsalted butter,
chilled and diced**
**1 tablespoon mixed peel,
very finely chopped**
3 tablespoons golden syrup

several baking sheets, greased

Makes about 20

Sift the flour into a mixing bowl with the salt, baking powder, bicarbonate of soda, ginger and mixed spice. (The combination of the two raising agents is what makes these biscuits crack.)

Stir in the sugar. Add the diced butter and rub the mixture together with your fingertips until it resembles fine crumbs. Stir in the mixed peel, then the syrup, to make a firm dough. (In cold weather, warm the syrup before adding it to the mixture.)

Using your hands, roll the dough into about 20 marble-sized balls. Space them well apart on the prepared baking sheets. Bake in a preheated oven at 200°C (400°F) Gas 6 for about 7 minutes or until golden.

Remove from the oven and let cool on the baking sheets for a couple of minutes until firm enough to transfer to a wire rack. Let cool completely, then store in an airtight container. Best eaten within 1 week, or freeze for up to 1 month.

lemon poppy seed biscuits

These crisp, light biscuits are great on their own or make a perfect complement to ice creams or fruit salad.

200 g plain flour

a pinch of salt

50 g icing sugar

50 g golden caster sugar

grated zest of 1 unwaxed lemon

2 teaspoons poppy seeds

120 g unsalted butter, chilled and diced

1 medium egg, beaten

several baking sheets, lightly greased

Makes about 26

Put the flour, salt, sugars, grated lemon zest and poppy seeds in a food processor and process until thoroughly mixed. Add the diced butter and process until the mixture resembles fine crumbs. Add the egg and process again until the dough clumps together.

Shape the dough into a log about 7 cm in diameter and wrap it in foil. Chill until hard – at least 2 hours, or up to 1 week. The mixture can be sliced and baked when needed.

When you are ready to cook the biscuits, slice the log into rounds about 5 mm thick. Place them slightly apart on the prepared baking sheets. Bake in a preheated oven at 180°C (350°F) Gas 4 until the edges are just beginning to turn golden brown – 10–12 minutes.

Remove from the oven and let cool on the baking sheets for a couple of minutes until firm enough to transfer to a wire rack. Let cool completely, then store in an airtight container and eat within 5 days, or freeze for up to 1 month.

SHORTBREAD

grasmere ginger shortbread

200 g plain flour

50 g fine oatmeal

1 teaspoon ground ginger

½ teaspoon bicarbonate of soda

125 g light brown muscovado sugar

1 piece of stem ginger in syrup, drained and roughly chopped

125 g unsalted butter, chilled and diced

a cake tin, 20 cm square, well greased

Makes 9 squares

A favourite shortbread recipe from the Lake District, with a strong ginger flavour and a crumbly topping, another with sugary speckles and a third with green unsalted pistachios.

Put the flour, oatmeal, ground ginger, bicarbonate of soda, sugar and stem ginger in a food processor and process until the mixture resembles coarse sand. Add the diced butter, then process until you have fine crumbs. Do not overwork the mixture – it should not form a dough.

Set aside 4 tablespoons of the crumbs. Tip the rest into the prepared tin and press into an even layer with the back of a spoon. Sprinkle the reserved crumbs on top.

Using a round-bladed knife, score the shortbread into 9 squares. Bake in a preheated oven at 180°C (350°F) Gas 4 for about 25 minutes or until the biscuits are just beginning to turn golden.

Remove the tin from the oven. Cut along the scored lines, but leave the shortbread to cool in the tin before turning out.

Store in an airtight container and eat within 1 week, or freeze for up to 1 month.

demerara shortbread

Put the butter in a bowl and beat until creamy, using a wooden spoon or electric mixer. Add the caster sugar and vanilla essence, if using, and beat until the mixture is light and fluffy.

Sift the flour with the rice flour, ground rice or cornflour and salt, then add to the butter mixture. Work the dough with your hands until it comes together, then knead gently for a few seconds.

Form the dough into a log shape 16 x 7.5 cm. Roll the log in the demerara sugar until evenly coated. Wrap in foil or greaseproof paper and chill until firm – about 20 minutes.

Unwrap the log and slice into 1 cm rounds. Arrange slightly apart on the prepared baking sheets, prick with a fork, then chill for about 15 minutes until firm.

Bake in a preheated oven at 180°C (350°F) Gas 4 for about 15 minutes until firm but not coloured. Remove the shortbread from the oven and let cool for a couple of minutes, then transfer to a wire rack. Let cool completely, then store in an airtight container. Best eaten within 1 week, or freeze for up to 1 month.

VARIATION

Pistachio Shortbread

Make the dough as in the main recipe, adding the pistachios but omitting the vanilla essence. Roll the dough out on a lightly floured work surface to 1 cm thick. Cut into rounds with a 7.5 cm round plain cutter, knead the trimmings together, re-roll and cut more rounds. Omit the demerara sugar. Arrange the rounds slightly apart on the prepared baking sheets, then chill for 15 minutes until firm. Bake as in the main recipe.

200 g unsalted butter, at room temperature

100 g golden caster sugar

2–3 drops real vanilla essence (optional)

260 g plain flour

40 g rice flour, ground rice or cornflour

a pinch of salt

3–4 tablespoons unrefined demerara sugar

several baking sheets, greased

Makes about 16

omit the vanilla essence and demerara sugar from the above ingredients

add 50 g shelled pistachio nuts, blanched, dried and roughly chopped

Makes about 14

chocolate shortbread

This rich, grainy shortbread is perfect served with vanilla ice cream.

200 g unsalted butter, at room temperature

100 g golden caster sugar

260 g plain flour

40 g cocoa powder

a good pinch of salt

extra caster sugar or icing sugar and cocoa, for sprinkling

a cake tin, 23 cm diameter, greased

Makes 12 triangles

Put the butter in a bowl and beat until creamy and light using a wooden spoon or electric mixer. Add the sugar and beat again until fluffy. Sift the flour with the cocoa and salt. Using a wooden spoon or your hands, work the dry ingredients into the butter mixture until the dough comes together. Knead gently for a couple of seconds, then press the dough into the prepared tin to make an even layer.

Cover and chill for 15 minutes. Prick the dough well with a fork and score into 12 triangles with a round-bladed knife.

Bake the shortbread in a preheated oven at 180°C (350°F) Gas 4 for 15–20 minutes – do not allow it to brown or it will taste bitter.

Remove from the oven, sprinkle with caster sugar or icing sugar and cocoa, then cut into 12 sections along the marked lines. Let cool before removing from the tin.

Store in an airtight container and eat within 1 week, or freeze for up to 1 month.

NUT BISCUITS

almond crescents

For crunchy texture and intense almond taste, use freshly ground and whole nuts – toasted first – and real almond essence.

120 g unsalted butter, at room temperature

2–3 drops real almond essence

60 g icing sugar, sifted, plus extra for dredging

a pinch of salt

90 g plain flour, sifted

120 g ground almonds

30 g whole almonds, lightly toasted, then chopped

several baking sheets, greased

Makes about 22

Put the butter and almond essence in a bowl and beat, using a wooden spoon or electric mixer, until light and creamy. Add the sifted sugar and mix slowly, then beat well until fluffy. Add the salt, flour and ground almonds, then mix thoroughly with a wooden spoon. Mix in the chopped toasted almonds and, if necessary, knead the dough gently, just enough to bring it together.

Do not overwork the dough – it should be quite firm. In warm weather, you may need to wrap it and chill it for 15–20 minutes to firm up the dough to the proper consistency.

Using your hands, roll heaped teaspoonfuls of the dough into sausages about 7 cm long, curving each into a crescent. Space well apart on the prepared baking sheets, then cook in a preheated oven at 170°C (325°F) Gas 3 for 15–18 minutes or until firm. They should still be pale, with only the tops slightly browned.

Remove from the oven and let cool on the sheets for 2 minutes, then dredge with icing sugar. Transfer to a wire rack to cool completely.

Store in an airtight container and eat within 1 week. This recipe does not freeze successfully.

lace biscuits

These delicate biscuits are perfect to serve with sorbet or little cups of strong, black, after-dinner coffee.

Melt the butter very gently in a small saucepan, then let it cool while you prepare the other ingredients.

Put the nuts, sugar and flour in a food processor and process until the nuts are finely ground. With the machine still running, pour in the cream and butter through the feed tube. Process until you have a soft dough.

Put heaped teaspoons of the mixture, spaced well apart, on the baking sheets. Flatten them with a fork, then bake in a preheated oven at 180°C (350°F) Gas 4 for 7–9 minutes or until they turn golden brown with slightly darker edges.

Remove from the oven and let cool on the baking sheets. Store the biscuits in an airtight container and eat within 4 days. They do not freeze well.

50 g unsalted butter

100 g chopped pecan nuts or walnut pieces

100 g golden caster sugar

3 tablespoons plain flour

2 tablespoons double cream

several baking sheets lined with non-stick baking parchment

Makes about 24

espresso walnut squares

For the best flavour, make the strongest possible espresso coffee, then let it cool before using.

140 g plain flour

a pinch of salt

140 g light brown muscovado sugar

90 g unsalted butter, chilled and diced

1 teaspoon baking powder

1 medium egg, beaten

3 tablespoons very strong espresso coffee, cold

1 tablespoon milk

60 g walnut pieces

a cake tin, 20 cm square, greased and base-lined

Makes 16 squares

Sift the flour, salt and sugar into a bowl. Add the diced butter and rub it in with your fingertips until the mixture resembles coarse crumbs. Set aside 4 tablespoons of the mixture. Add the baking powder to the rest and mix well. Put the egg, coffee and milk in a separate bowl and mix, then stir into the flour mixture. When thoroughly mixed, add 45 g of the walnuts.

Spoon the mixture into the prepared tin and smooth the surface.

Mix the remaining nuts with the reserved crumbs and scatter over the top.

Bake in a preheated oven at 180°C (350°F) Gas 4 for 20–25 minutes until golden brown and firm to the touch.

Remove from the oven, let cool for 1–2 minutes, then run a palette knife around the edges of the tin to loosen the cake before carefully turning out on to a wire rack.

Leave until completely cold before cutting into 16 squares. Store in an airtight container and eat within 4 days, or freeze for up to 1 month.

mocha macaroons

Put the chopped chocolate in a heatproof bowl, set it over a saucepan of steaming, not boiling, water and melt gently. Remove the bowl from the heat and stir until smooth. Let cool slightly.

Put the egg whites in a separate bowl and whisk using a hand whisk or electric mixer until they form stiff peaks. Gradually whisk in the sugar, then fold in the almonds, coffee and melted chocolate.

When well mixed, put heaped teaspoonfuls of the mixture, spaced well apart, on the prepared baking sheets. Spread into circles about 6 cm across, then sprinkle with the almonds.

Bake in a preheated oven at 150°C (300°F) Gas 2 for about 25 minutes or until firm.

Remove from the oven, let cool slightly, then peel off the parchment or remove the macaroons from the greased sheet. Transfer them to a wire rack and let cool completely.

Store in an airtight container and eat within 1 week. These macaroons do not freeze well.

75 g plain chocolate, chopped

2 medium egg whites

200 g golden caster sugar

125 g ground almonds

1 tablespoon strong espresso coffee

sliced, split or slivered almonds, to finish

several baking sheets, well greased or lined with non-stick baking parchment

Makes 18

Use sugar-free peanut butter in this recipe or the biscuits will be much too sweet.

peanut butter and jelly biscuit sandwiches

275 g crunchy peanut butter

150 g golden caster sugar

2–3 drops real vanilla essence

1 large egg, beaten

about 4 tablespoons raspberry jam or redcurrant jelly, for the filling

several baking sheets, well greased

Makes about 12 sandwiches

Put the peanut butter and sugar in a bowl and beat well with a wooden spoon. Beat in the vanilla essence and the egg. The dough should be very stiff.

Divide the dough into 24 pieces and roll them into balls with your hands. Space the balls well apart on the baking sheets, then flatten with a fork.

Bake in a preheated oven at 180°C (350°F) Gas 4 for 12–15 minutes or until golden brown. Remove the biscuits from the oven and leave them on the baking sheets for a few minutes to firm up, then transfer to a wire rack to cool completely.

Sandwich pairs of biscuits together with a little jam or jelly.

Store in an airtight container and eat within 1 week. The biscuits can be frozen for up to 1 month, but they must be frozen without the jam or jelly filling.

NOTE: This recipe is suitable for people on gluten-free diets and for serving during Passover.

macadamia nut white chocolate crumbles

200 g plain flour

a pinch of salt

½ teaspoon baking powder

175 g unsalted butter, at room temperature

100 g golden caster sugar

1 medium egg, lightly beaten

½ teaspoon real vanilla essence

150 g good quality white chocolate, coarsely chopped

75 g unsalted macadamia nuts, coarsely chopped

several baking sheets, lightly greased

Makes about 24

An elegant combination of white nuts, white chocolate and a white biscuit mixture.

Sift the flour, salt and baking powder into a bowl.

Put the butter and sugar in a separate bowl and cream until fluffy using a wooden spoon or electric mixer.

Beat the egg into the butter mixture and, when thoroughly mixed, stir in the flour mixture using a large metal spoon. When no streaks are visible, stir in the vanilla, chocolate and nuts.

Put tablespoons of the mixture, spaced well apart, on the prepared baking sheets. Bake in a preheated oven at 180°C (350°F) Gas 4 for 10–12 minutes until firm but not coloured. Leave the biscuits to cool on the sheets for 1 minute, then transfer to a wire rack to cool completely.

Store in an airtight container and eat within 5 days. These biscuits do not freeze well.

Walnuts make wonderful biscuits, but pecans or hazelnuts will also work well in this recipe.

walnut biscuits

70 g walnut pieces, chopped

90 g unsalted butter,
at room temperature

80 g golden caster sugar

80 g unrefined demerara sugar

1 large egg, beaten

½ teaspoon real vanilla essence

250 g self-raising flour

several baking sheets, greased

Makes 24

Walnuts can sometimes be very bitter and can also turn rancid very quickly when exposed to air, so taste one first before using them in this recipe.

Using a wooden spoon or electric mixer, beat the butter until soft and creamy. Gradually beat in the sugars and continue beating for another 2 minutes.

Beat in the egg a little at a time, then stir in the vanilla essence, flour and nuts. Work the mixture with your hands until it comes together into a firm dough. Again using your hands, roll the dough into 24 walnut-sized balls.

Put the balls, spaced well apart, on the baking sheets, then flatten with a fork. Bake in a preheated oven at 180°C (350°F) Gas 4 for about 10 minutes or until golden and firm.

Remove from the oven, leave on the baking sheets for a couple of minutes to firm up, then transfer to a wire rack to cool completely.

Store in an airtight container and eat within 1 week, or freeze for up to 1 month.

AROUND THE WORLD

almond biscotti

These twice-baked biscotti from Tuscany are served after dinner with fresh fruit and a glass of sweet Vin Santo wine for dipping and sipping.

130 g blanched almonds

250 g plain flour

125 g vanilla caster sugar, if available, or caster sugar

¾ teaspoon baking powder

2 large eggs, plus 1 yolk

½ teaspoon real almond essence or vanilla essence

a baking sheet, greased

Makes about 20

Put the almonds on a heatproof dish and toast in a preheated oven at 180°C (350°F) Gas 4 for 10–12 minutes until lightly browned. Let cool, then roughly chop 100 g of the nuts and set aside. Leave the oven on.

Put the remaining nuts in a food processor and grind to a fine powder.

Put the ground almonds in a bowl, add the flour, sugar and baking powder and mix. Make a well in the centre. Beat the eggs with the yolk and the almond or vanilla essence and pour into the well in the flour. Gradually work the flour mixture into the eggs, then add the chopped almonds. Knead very well to bring the dough together – do not add any extra liquid.

Divide the dough in half and shape each piece into a flat log about 26 x 6 x 1.5 cm. Place the logs well apart on the baking sheet. Bake at 180°C (350°F) Gas 4 for about 25 minutes until golden and firm to the touch. Remove from the oven and let cool for about 5 minutes. Reduce the oven temperature to 170°C (325°F) Gas 3.

Transfer the logs to a chopping board and using a serrated knife, carefully cut them diagonally into slices about 1.5 cm thick. Arrange the slices, cut side up, on the baking sheet and bake for 10–12 minutes at the reduced temperature until golden and crisp.

Remove the biscotti from the oven, leave for 5 minutes to firm up, then transfer to a wire rack to cool. Store in an airtight container and eat within 2 weeks.

cinnamon and raisin biscotti

Traditional biscotti, flavoured with fennel seeds, are served as a digestif. This is a modern variation.

Put the almonds on a heatproof dish and toast in a preheated oven at 180°C (350°F) Gas 4 for 10–12 minutes until lightly browned. Let cool and leave whole.

Put the egg, sugar and vanilla essence in a bowl and whisk by hand or with an electric mixer until very thick and pale (ribbons of mixture should trail from the whisk as you lift it out of the bowl). Sift the flour, baking powder, salt and cinnamon on to a piece of greaseproof paper, then sift again into the bowl with the egg mixture. Stir until thoroughly mixed, then stir in the raisins and almonds. Turn the dough out on to the prepared baking sheet and shape into a flat log about 26 x 6 x 1.5 cm.

Bake the log in a preheated oven at 180°C (350°F) Gas 4 for 20–25 minutes or until golden brown. Remove from the oven, let cool for about 5 minutes or until firm, then transfer to a chopping board. Reduce the oven temperature to 170°C (325°F) Gas 3.

With a serrated knife, carefully cut the log diagonally into slices about 1 cm thick. Arrange the slices on the sheet and bake again for 10–15 minutes or until golden. Remove the biscotti from the oven and let cool for 5 minutes, then transfer to a wire rack to cool completely. Store in an airtight container and eat within 2 weeks.

50 g whole blanched almonds

1 large egg

100 g golden caster sugar

1 teaspoon real vanilla essence

130 g plain flour

½ teaspoon baking powder

a pinch of salt

¾ teaspoon ground cinnamon

50 g raisins

a baking sheet, well greased

Makes about 20

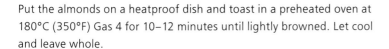

Tuiles are the perfect accompaniment to
ice cream, creamy puddings or fruit salads.

orange tuiles

Put the egg whites in a spotlessly clean, grease-free, non-plastic
bowl. Using a hand or electric whisk, whisk slowly at first, then
increase the speed until the egg whites form stiff peaks. Gradually
whisk in the sugar, then the cooled melted butter and finally the
sifted flour. If you use an electric mixer, keep it on low speed.

Gently stir in the grated orange zest and the liqueur, if using.

Spoon 1 teaspoon of the mixture on to a prepared baking sheet
and spread it into a thin disc about 10 cm across. Bake it in
a preheated oven at 180°C (350°F) Gas 4 for about 5 minutes
or until it turns a very pale gold.

Remove from the oven and, using a palette knife, immediately
loosen it from the sheet and drape it over a rolling pin. It will
harden very rapidly into a U-shape. Remove and set aside. Once
you have the knack, bake the tuiles 2 at a time.

Store the tuiles in an airtight container, and eat within 2 days –
humidity or damp makes them uncurl, so store with care.
These biscuits are not suitable for freezing.

**2 medium egg whites,
at room temperature**

120 g golden caster sugar

**60 g unsalted butter,
melted and cooled**

60 g plain flour, sifted

**grated zest of
1 unwaxed orange**

**1 teaspoon orange
liqueur (optional)**

several baking sheets, greased

Makes about 18

danish biscuits

A hint of cinnamon makes these delicate, lacy biscuits an excellent match for ice cream or creamy summertime puddings.

150 g unsalted butter
150 g porridge oats
230 g golden caster sugar
2 medium eggs, beaten
1 tablespoon plain flour
2 teaspoons baking powder
1 teaspoon ground cinnamon

several baking sheets,
well greased or lined with
non-stick baking parchment

Makes about 24

Put the butter in a medium saucepan and melt gently. Remove the pan from the heat and stir in the porridge oats. When thoroughly mixed, add the sugar, eggs, flour, baking powder and ground cinnamon and mix well.

These biscuits are best baked in batches of three. (Cook the batches on one baking sheet while the other is cooling down).

Space 3 mounds – each about 1 heaped teaspoonful of the mixture – well apart on a baking sheet.

Bake in a preheated oven at 180°C (350°F) Gas 4 for 5–7 minutes or until golden brown.

Remove from the oven and using a spatula, immediately lift the baked biscuits off the sheet and let cool upside down on a wire rack. Repeat the process until all the mixture is used.

These biscuits quickly lose their crispness in damp or humid conditions, so store carefully in an airtight container and eat within 4 days. They do not freeze well.

irish whiskey fingers

Soak the fruit in whiskey the night before baking – Irish whiskey gives the best flavour, but Scotch is very good too.

Using a vegetable peeler, pare off the zest of the lemon and put it in a small bowl. Add the sultanas, then pour over the whiskey. Cover the bowl tightly and leave overnight.

Using a wooden spoon or electric mixer, beat the butter until creamy. Beat in the sugar and continue beating until the mixture is very light and fluffy. Beat in the egg yolks one at a time.

Remove the lemon zest from the whiskey mixture, then add the sultanas and whiskey to the cake mixture, carefully folding them in using a metal spoon.

In another bowl, whisk the egg whites until they form stiff peaks, then fold them into the mixture in 3 batches alternately with batches of the flour.

Spoon the mixture into the prepared tin and smooth the surface. Sprinkle with the demerara sugar, then bake in a preheated oven at 180°C (350°F) Gas 4 for about 25 minutes or until just firm to the touch.

Remove from the oven, let rest in the tin for about 5 minutes, then carefully unmould the cake on to a wire rack. Let cool completely, then cut into 10 fingers.

Store in an airtight container and eat within 1 week, or freeze for up to 1 month.

1 unwaxed lemon

100 g sultanas

80 ml whiskey

130 g unsalted butter, at room temperature

130 g golden caster sugar

2 large eggs, separated

130 g self-raising flour

1–2 tablespoons demerara sugar

a cake tin, 18 cm square, greased and base-lined

Cuts into 10

sablés

Put the flour, salt, icing sugar and diced butter in a food processor and process until the mixture resembles fine sand. Add the egg yolks and vanilla essence and process again until the mixture comes together as a firm dough. Take it out of the processor, wrap it and chill for 15 minutes.

Roll out the chilled dough on a lightly floured work surface to about 5 mm thick. Cut out rounds with the fluted cutter and space them slightly apart on the baking sheets.

Knead the trimmings together, roll again, cut more rounds and arrange them on the sheets. Brush the rounds very lightly with beaten egg, then chill for 15 minutes.

Brush again with the egg glaze, prick all over with a fork, then mark with the prongs to make a neat pattern.

Bake the biscuits in a preheated oven at 180°C (350°F) Gas 4 for 12–15 minutes or until golden brown. Remove the biscuits from the oven, leave them on the baking sheets for a few seconds to firm up, then carefully transfer to a wire rack to cool completely.

Store in an airtight container and eat within 1 week, or freeze for up to 1 month.

200 g plain flour

a pinch of salt

80 g icing sugar

130 g unsalted butter, chilled and diced

3 egg yolks

½ teaspoon real vanilla essence

1 egg, beaten, to glaze

a fluted biscuit cutter, 9 cm diameter

several baking sheets, greased

Makes about 10

For authentic flavour, make these vanilla-scented French biscuits with unsalted best quality butter.

FINGERS & BARS

soured cream cardamom squares

Sift the flour with the bicarbonate of soda, salt and ground cardamom, then set aside.

Using a wooden spoon or electric mixer, beat the butter until creamy. Gradually beat in the sugar and continue beating until the mixture is very light and fluffy. Add the eggs 1 at a time, beating well after each addition. Using a large metal spoon, fold in the flour mixture in 3 batches, alternating with the soured cream.

Spoon the mixture into the prepared cake tin and smooth the surface. Bake in a preheated oven at 180°C (350°F) Gas 4 for about 45 minutes or until golden brown and firm to the touch.

Remove from the oven, loosen the edges with a round-bladed knife, then turn on to a wire rack to cool completely. When completely cold, cut into 9 squares and dust with icing sugar.

Store in an airtight container and eat within 1 week, or freeze for up to 1 month.

250 g self-raising flour

½ teaspoon bicarbonate of soda

a pinch of salt

¼ teaspoon ground cardamom

**170 g unsalted butter,
at room temperature**

250 g golden caster sugar

3 large eggs

150 ml soured cream

icing sugar, for dusting

*a cake tin, 20 cm square,
greased and base-lined*

Makes 9

If using whole cardamom, crack the pods, remove the seeds and crush them with a mortar and pestle.

mincemeat crumble

Sift the flour, salt and mixed spice into a bowl. Rub in the diced butter with your fingertips until the mixture resembles fine crumbs. Stir in the sugar, diced apple, dried fruit and peel. Put the egg and the milk in a separate bowl and mix. Add this to the flour mixture and stir to make a soft dough.

Transfer the dough to the prepared tin and smooth the surface. Sprinkle with the demerara sugar.

Bake in a preheated oven at 200°C (400°F) Gas 6 for about 20 minutes or until firm and golden. Remove from the oven, let cool for 1 minute, then cut into 9 squares.

Let cool completely, then store in an airtight container. Eat within 4 days, or freeze for up to 1 month.

VARIATION

Dried Fruit, Pineapple and Apricot Crumble

Omit the apple and substitute 140 g of one of the luxury dried fruit mixtures, containing pineapple and apricot, that are often available around holiday time.

225 g self-raising flour

a pinch of salt

½ teaspoon ground mixed spice

85 g unsalted butter, chilled and diced

85 g unrefined demerara sugar

1 medium apple, peeled, cored and diced

100 g mixed dried fruit and peel

1 large egg

4 tablespoons milk

1–2 tablespoons demerara sugar, for sprinkling

a cake tin, 20 cm square, greased

Makes 9

Crisp, tart, eating apples are best for this quick and easy crumble.

pecan spice bars

90 g unsalted butter,
at room temperature

3 tablespoons golden syrup

1 large egg

180 g self-raising flour

a pinch of salt

¼ teaspoon grated nutmeg

½ teaspoon mixed ground spice

½ teaspoon ground cinnamon

¼ teaspoon ground ginger

90 g coarsely ground pecan nuts

1½ tablespoons milk

Spicy Pecan Topping

2 tablespoons flour

2 tablespoons muscovado sugar

¼ teaspoon grated nutmeg

¼ teaspoon grated ginger

30 g unsalted butter, diced

30 g pecan halves

*a cake tin, 20 cm square,
greased and lined*

Makes 15

An excellent combination of moist sponge base and crunchy topping of nuts and spices.

Using a wooden spoon or electric mixer, cream the butter until light and fluffy. Beat in the golden syrup, then gradually beat in the egg.

Sift the flour with the salt and spices, then stir into the butter mixture. Add the ground pecans and milk and stir well. Spoon the mixture into the prepared tin and smooth the surface.

To make the topping, put the flour, sugar and spices in a bowl and mix. Rub in the diced butter with your fingertips to make small clumps of dough. Stir in the pecans.

Scatter the clumps over the base mixture in the tin, then bake in a preheated oven at 180°C (350°F) Gas 4 for 25–30 minutes until firm to the touch.

Remove the cake in its paper lining from the tin. Let cool, then slice into 15 pieces. Store in an airtight container and eat within 1 week, or freeze for up to 1 month.

Use only genuine maple syrup for a more intense flavour.

maple syrup pecan flapjacks

Put the butter, sugar and syrup in a medium saucepan and heat gently, stirring occasionally, until the sugar has dissolved. Remove the pan from the heat, stir in the oats and nuts and mix well.

Transfer the mixture to the prepared tin and spread evenly, pressing down lightly. Using a sharp knife, score the mixture into 10 rectangles.

Bake in a preheated oven at 150°C (300°F) Gas 2 for 25–30 minutes or until golden.

Remove from the oven and cut along the scored lines. Do not remove the flapjacks from the tin until they are completely cold. Store in an airtight container and eat within 1 week, or freeze for up to 1 month.

VARIATIONS

Golden Syrup Flapjacks

Omit the pecan nuts and maple syrup and use 1 tablespoon golden syrup instead. Instead of the nuts, add one of the following: 30 g raisins, 30 g chocolate pieces, 1 teaspoon ground ginger, 40 g each of chopped dates and walnut pieces, 40 g chopped almonds and a few drops almond essence, or 40 g chopped mixed nuts with 40 g ready-to-eat dried apricots.

150 g unsalted butter

120 g light brown muscovado sugar

1 tablespoon maple syrup

180 g porridge oats

70 g pecan nuts, roughly chopped

a cake tin, 18 cm square, well greased

Makes 10

tangy lemon bars

125 g plain flour

a pinch of salt

35 g icing sugar

100 g unsalted butter, chilled and diced

3 drops real vanilla essence

Lemon Topping

2 medium eggs

170 g golden caster sugar

grated zest and freshly squeezed juice of 1 large unwaxed lemon

1 tablespoon plain flour

½ teaspoon bicarbonate of soda

icing sugar, for dusting (optional)

a cake tin, 20 cm square, well greased

Makes 12

Put the flour, salt and icing sugar in a food processor and process to mix. Add the butter and the vanilla essence and process until the mixture comes together to make a firm dough.

Press the dough into the base of the prepared tin to make an even layer. Prick well with a fork and, if the weather is very warm, chill for 15 minutes.

Bake in a preheated oven at 180°C (350°F) Gas 4 for 12–15 minutes until firm and slightly golden but not browned.

Remove from the oven and let cool in the tin while making the topping.

Using an electric mixer or whisk, whisk the eggs in a bowl until frothy. Gradually whisk in the sugar and continue until the mixture is thick and foamy. Whisk in the lemon zest and juice, then the flour and bicarbonate of soda. Pour the mixture over the base and bake for 20–25 minutes until it turns golden brown.

Remove from the oven and let cool in the tin, then divide into 12 rectangles. Dust with icing sugar before serving, if liked. Store in an airtight container and eat within 4 days. This recipe does not freeze well.

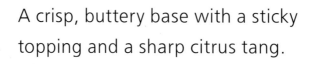

A crisp, buttery base with a sticky topping and a sharp citrus tang.

flavoured
breads

homemade bread

With exotic, ever-changing variety in our supermarkets, why bake bread? It saves money, of course, and has a taste and texture worlds away from even the best you can buy. You need no special talent – just flour, yeast, salt, water, a baking sheet, an oven and some time.

Much of the flavour in home-made bread comes from quality flours. Spelt, for instance, is higher in protein and has a greater concentration of vitamins and minerals than ordinary flours. Malted brown flour makes a light, textured loaf with nutty pieces of wheat. Strong white bread flour can be mixed with other flours, such as rye, to lighten them. Coarse stoneground whole-wheat makes a chewy, rough-textured loaf. Other ways of flavouring dough come from additions such as poppy seeds, olives, herbs, walnuts or bacon.

Rising agents used in breads include easy-blend dried yeast and fresh yeast. When wrapped, fresh yeast can be refrigerated for 1 week or frozen for 1 month. When you make bread, dried yeast is mixed with flour; fresh yeast with liquid, usually water.

The amount of salt is crucial. Add too little and the dough will rise too fast, then collapse; while too much will inhibit the effectiveness of, or even kill, the yeast.

The quantity of liquid needed to form the dough depends on the condition of the flours, the type of flavourings and even the weather. The ideal texture is soft but not sticky, add extra flour or water as necessary.

Thorough kneading is vital. It develops gluten, the substance in the flour that acts as scaffolding to support the bubbles of carbon dioxide from the yeast. It also ensures that the yeast is evenly distributed through the dough so it rises uniformly. Knead by hand or in a mixer fitted with a dough hook, but not in a food processor.

When dough is left to rise uncovered it forms a dry crust, which results in hard lumps in the baked loaf. So always cover your rising dough with a damp tea towel or a large polythene bag. Too little rising time produces a heavy, small loaf. Too much is even worse: dough seriously distended by too long or too quick a rise will collapse in the oven.

Preheating the oven is important. A hot oven kills yeast quickly and prevents over-rising. All ovens are different, so check shelf positions in your handbook and take my cooking times as guidelines, particularly with fan ovens. To test whether a loaf is cooked, unmould it and knock it on the bottom with your knuckles: it should sound hollow. If it doesn't, replace and bake for 5 minutes more before testing again.

Baked bread should be removed from the sheet or tin and cooled on a wire rack to help form a good crust. For best results, slice bread only when it's really cool.

MEDITERRANEAN
BREAD

bacon and walnut fougasses

4 tablespoons olive oil,
plus extra for greasing

85 g rindless bacon, finely diced

60 g walnut pieces,
roughly chopped

700 g unbleached white
bread flour, plus extra
for dusting

2 teaspoons sea salt

15 g fresh yeast, crumbled*

300 ml lukewarm water

1 medium egg, beaten

several baking sheets, greased

Makes 8 pieces

**To use easy-blend dried yeast, add
one 7 g sachet to the flour when
you add the salt.*

Heat 1 tablespoon oil in a frying pan, add the bacon and fry until golden and crisp, but not hard. Drain on kitchen paper, then mix well with the walnuts.

Put the flour and salt in a large bowl, mix well, then make a well in the centre. Put the yeast and water in a small bowl and cream to a smooth liquid. Tip into the well in the flour, then mix in the egg and remaining olive oil. Gradually work in the flour to make a soft but not sticky dough. If there are crumbs in the bottom of the bowl, add water, 1 tablespoon at a time, until the dough comes together. If the dough sticks to your fingers, work in more flour, 1 tablespoon at a time.

Take out the dough and transfer it to a lightly floured work surface. Knead thoroughly for 10 minutes until the dough feels smooth, very elastic and silky.

Put the dough in a lightly oiled bowl and turn the dough over so the entire surface is lightly coated with oil.

Cover with a damp tea towel and let rise at room temperature until doubled in size – about 1½ hours. Uncover, knock back the dough, then transfer it to a lightly floured work surface. Knead in the bacon and nuts until evenly distributed.

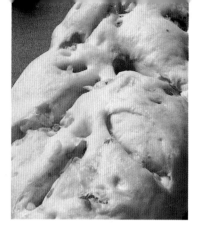

Weigh the dough and divide into 8 equal parts. Using a rolling pin, roll each piece into an oval about 21 x 12 x 1 cm. With a sharp knife, cut about 8 slits in a herringbone pattern in each oval. Arrange them, spaced well apart, on the baking sheets. Lightly cover the baking sheets with a damp tea towel and let rise at cool to normal room temperature until doubled in size – about 45 minutes.

Uncover, lightly brush with oil, then bake in a preheated oven at 200°C (400°F) Gas 6 for 15–20 minutes until golden brown. Remove from the oven and transfer to a wire rack to cool.

VARIATION

Salami Fougasses

Omit the bacon and walnuts. Skin a 100 g piece of saucisson sec or salami, chop finely and add after the first rising. Proceed as in the main recipe.

These attractive, individual loaves come from Provence where, these days, they are made plain or flavoured with charcuterie, olives, herbs or even candied fruit. Use top-quality bacon, such as *poitrine fumée* or dry-cured, thick-cut smoked streaky.

focaccia with rosemary and sea salt

This dough has three risings. For an open, light texture, don't overload with olive oil.

Put the yeast and half the water in a small bowl and cream to a smooth liquid. Add 3 tablespoons oil and the remaining water. Add the salt, chopped rosemary and half the flour. Beat into the liquid with your hand. When mixed, work in enough of the remaining flour to make a soft but not sticky dough.

Transfer the dough to a lightly floured work surface and knead for 10 minutes until very smooth and silky (or for up to 5 minutes at low speed in a mixer fitted with a dough hook). Put the dough in a lightly oiled bowl and turn the dough over so the entire surface is coated with oil. Cover with a damp tea towel and let rise at cool to normal room temperature until doubled in size – about 2 hours.

Uncover, knock back the dough, then transfer it to a lightly floured work surface. Shape it into a rectangle. Press into the base of the tin, pushing into the corners and patting out to make an even layer. Cover with a damp tea towel and let rise as before until almost doubled in height – 45–60 minutes.

Flour your fingertips and press into the risen dough to make dimples 1 cm deep. Cover with a damp tea towel and let rise again until doubled in height – about 1 hour. Uncover the dough, press sprigs of rosemary into the dimples and fill them with olive oil. Sprinkle with sea salt and bake in a preheated oven at 220°C (425°F) Gas 7 for 20–25 minutes until golden brown. Remove from the oven, lift the loaf out of the tin and transfer it to a wire rack to cool.

15 g fresh yeast, crumbled*

**280 ml water,
at room temperature**

**6–7 tablespoons extra virgin
olive oil, plus extra for greasing**

2 teaspoons sea salt

**2 tablespoons finely chopped
fresh rosemary, plus extra sprigs**

**about 500 g unbleached
white bread flour, plus extra
for dusting**

2 teaspoons coarse sea salt

*a roasting or baking tin,
about 25 x 35 cm, greased*

Makes 1 loaf

**To use easy-blend dried yeast, add
one 7 g sachet with the chopped
rosemary. Put all the liquid in the
bowl at once and proceed with
the recipe.*

Two variations on the main focaccia recipe.

focaccia with pancetta

Additional Ingredients

100–150 g pancetta or streaky bacon

about 3 tablespoons extra virgin olive oil

sea salt and coarsely ground black pepper

a roasting or baking tin, about 25 x 35 cm, greased

Makes 1 loaf

Follow the recipe on page 188, omitting the fresh rosemary and sea salt.

During the first rising, grill the pancetta or bacon, discarding any rind and small pieces of bone. Drain on kitchen paper and let cool, then chop finely and sprinkle with coarsely ground black pepper.

Knock back the risen dough and knead in the pancetta or bacon. Roll out the dough to fit the tin, then proceed as in the main recipe, drizzling with olive oil to fill the dimples and sprinkling with sea salt and coarsely ground black pepper. Bake, then let cool, as in the main recipe.

cherry tomato focaccia with basil

Follow the recipe on page 188, omitting the fresh rosemary and sea salt.

Cut the tomatoes in half and strip the leaves from a large bunch of fresh basil. Just after making the dimples, push a basil leaf into each hollow, then half a tomato, cut side up. Cover the dough and let rise as before until doubled in height – about 1 hour.

Drizzle with olive oil to moisten the tomatoes and sprinkle with sea salt and pepper. Bake, then let cool, as in the main recipe.

Additional Ingredients

150 g ripe fresh cherry tomatoes

a large bunch of fresh basil

4 tablespoons extra virgin olive oil

sea salt and freshly ground black pepper

a roasting or baking tin, about 25 x 35 cm, greased

Makes 1 loaf

The longer the olives marinate in the flavoured oil, the better. For a sharper taste, use green olives.

italian ciabatta with olives and thyme

150 g black olives, preferably kalamata, pitted

150 ml virgin olive oil

strip of unwaxed lemon zest

3 teaspoons chopped fresh thyme leaves

700 g unbleached white bread flour, plus extra for sprinkling

35 g fresh yeast, crumbled*

450 ml cold water

2½ teaspoons sea salt

2 baking sheets, well greased

Makes 2 loaves

*This recipe is not successful when made with dried yeast.

Put the olives in a bowl and add the olive oil, lemon zest and thyme. Cover and let marinate for 3–4 hours or overnight.

Put 500 g flour in a large bowl and make a well in the centre.

Put the yeast and 100 ml of the water in a small bowl and cream to a smooth liquid. Pour into the well, then add the remaining water. Mix to a sticky dough, almost like batter.

Cover with a damp tea towel and let rise at normal room temperature for 3–4 hours. It should grow to about 3 times its original size. Check occasionally to make sure the dough has not stuck to the tea towel. Knock back the dough.

Strain the olives, discard the lemon zest and reserve the oil. Mix the oil and salt into the dough, then gradually work in the remaining flour to make a soft, sticky dough. Cut in half and put 1 portion in another bowl. Mix half the olives into each portion.

Cover with damp tea towels and let rise as before until doubled in size – about 1 hour.

Tip the dough on to a baking sheet and shape into 2 rectangles 2.5 cm thick. Push the olives back into the dough, sprinkle with flour and let rise uncovered at room temperature until doubled in size – about 1 hour. Bake in a preheated oven at 220°C (425°F) Gas 7 for 30 minutes until the loaves are brown and sound hollow when tapped underneath. Remove from the oven and transfer to a wire rack to cool.

olive oil bread

Put the flour and salt in a large bowl, mix, then make a well in the centre.

Put the yeast and 3 tablespoons of the water in a small bowl and cream to a smooth liquid. Pour into the well in the flour, then add most of the remaining water. Quickly mix the flour into the liquid, then pour in the oil and continue mixing until the dough comes together. Gradually add the rest of the water, if necessary – the dough should be fairly soft, but should hold its shape and not stick to your fingers.

Transfer the dough to a lightly floured work surface. Knead thoroughly for 10 minutes until the dough is elastic and silky smooth. Put the dough in a lightly oiled bowl and turn the dough over so the entire surface is lightly coated with oil. Cover with a damp tea towel and let rise at cool to normal room temperature until doubled in size – about 2 hours.

Take the dough out and transfer to a floured work surface. Do not knock down or knead, but gently shape the dough into a 55-cm long sausage. Join the ends to make a ring. Transfer to the prepared baking sheet, cover with a damp tea towel and let rise as before until almost doubled in size – about 1 hour.

Uncover the loaf, dust with flour and bake in a preheated oven at 230°C (450°F) Gas 8 for 10 minutes. Reduce the oven temperature to 190°C (375°F) Gas 5 and bake for another 20 minutes or until it sounds hollow when tapped underneath. Remove from the oven and transfer to a wire rack to cool.

1 kg unbleached white bread flour, plus extra for dusting

3½ teaspoons sea salt

20 g fresh yeast, crumbled*

about 600 ml water, at room temperature

100 ml extra virgin olive oil

vegetable oil, for greasing

a large baking sheet, lightly greased

Makes 1 large loaf

*To use easy-blend dried yeast, add 10 g (1½ x 7 g sachets) to the flour with the salt, then proceed with the recipe.

For this open-textured loaf, use well-flavoured olive oil and good quality, stoneground, organic flour.

SPICES & SEEDS

saffron plait

1 heaped teaspoon saffron strands

150 ml warm water

700 g strong white bread flour, plus extra for dusting

3 teaspoons sea salt

1 teaspoon golden caster sugar

25 g unsalted butter, chilled and diced

15 g fresh yeast, crumbled*

300 ml skimmed milk, at room temperature

1 medium egg, beaten

vegetable oil, for greasing

1 egg beaten with a good pinch of salt, to glaze

a large baking sheet, greased

Makes 1 large loaf

*To use easy-blend dried yeast, add one 7 g sachet to the flour with the salt and sugar, then proceed with the recipe.

Put the saffron on a heatproof plate and toast in a preheated oven at 180°C (350°F) Gas 4, without burning, for 10–15 minutes. Crumble it into a bowl, then add the warm water, stir, cover and let soak overnight.

Next day, put the flour, salt and sugar in a large bowl and mix. Add the diced butter and rub it in with your fingertips until the mixture looks like breadcrumbs. Make a well in the centre, then pour in the saffron and its soaking water.

Put the yeast and milk in a small bowl and cream until smooth. Stir in the egg, then pour into the well in the flour. Work the mixture to form a fairly firm, soft dough. If any dry crumbs remain, work in extra milk, 1 tablespoon at a time. If the dough sticks to your fingers, work in extra flour, 1 tablespoon at a time.

Transfer the dough to a floured work surface and knead thoroughly for 10 minutes (or 5 minutes at low speed in a mixer fitted with a dough hook). The dough should be very elastic and silky smooth. Put into a lightly greased bowl and turn it over so the entire surface is lightly coated with oil. Cover with a damp tea towel and let rise at normal room temperature until doubled in size – about 1½ hours.

Uncover the dough, knock it back with your knuckles, then transfer it to a floured work surface. The dough should be pliable but not soft and should hold its shape. If not, knead in a little more flour.

Weigh the dough, divide it into 3–4 equal pieces and plait as described below. Cover with a damp tea towel and let rise at a cool temperature until almost doubled in size – 1–1½ hours. Don't let it over-rise or become too soft in a warm place or it will spread.

Uncover the plait, brush the top with the egg glaze, then bake in a preheated oven at 230°C (450°F) Gas 8 for 15 minutes until golden. Reduce the oven temperature to 200°C (400°F) Gas 6 and bake for 20–30 minutes until it sounds hollow when tapped underneath. Remove from the oven and transfer to a wire rack to cool.

To make a 3-strand plait

Using your hands, roll 3 pieces of dough into ropes 40 cm long. Put the 3 ropes on the baking sheet, then plait loosely together. Avoid overstretching the dough. Tuck the ends under to give a good shape.

To make a 4-strand plait

Using your hands, roll 4 pieces of dough into ropes 33 cm long and 2.5 cm thick. Pinch them firmly together at one end, then arrange vertically in front of you, side by side, slightly apart, with the join at the top. Run the far-left strand under the 2 middle ones, then back over the last it went under. Run the far-right strand under the twisted 2 in the middle, then back over the last it went under. Repeat until all the dough is plaited. Pinch the ends together at the bottom. Transfer to a baking sheet, tucking the ends under to give a neat shape.

Saffron gives a rich gold colour and a deep, aromatic flavour to bread dough. The longer the saffron is soaked, the better.

vanilla challah

Made to celebrate the Jewish sabbath, this rich, sweet bread can be flavoured with honey, saffron or spices.

Put the milk, sugar and vanilla pod in a small saucepan and heat until just steaming. Cover and set aside while the milk cools to lukewarm. Remove the pod and scrape the seeds into the milk.

Put the yeast and milk in a small bowl and cream to a smooth liquid.

Put the flour and salt in a bowl and mix. Make a well in the centre, pour the yeast liquid, butter and eggs into the well, then mix. Work in the flour to make a soft but not sticky dough. If too dry, add lukewarm water, 1 tablespoon at a time. If sticky and soft, work in flour, 1 tablespoon at a time. Transfer the dough to a floured work surface and knead for 10 minutes until silky and elastic.

Return to the washed and oiled bowl and turn until the entire surface is lightly coated with oil. Cover with a damp tea towel and let rise in a cool spot until doubled in size – 1½–2 hours.

Knock back the dough, cover and let rise as before – about 45 minutes. Knock back again and knead in the bowl for 1 minute. Let rest in the bowl, covered with the tea towel, for 5 minutes.

Divide and plait the dough as described on page 199. Brush with 2 thin coats of egg-yolk glaze and bake in a preheated oven at 220°C (425°F) Gas 7 for 10 minutes. Remove from the oven, glaze again, then reduce the oven temperature to 190°C (375°F) Gas 5 and bake for 30 minutes or until the loaf is golden brown and sounds hollow when tapped underneath. Remove from the oven and transfer to a wire rack to cool.

230 ml skimmed milk

2 tablespoons golden caster sugar

1 vanilla pod, split lengthways

15 g fresh yeast, crumbled*

700 g unbleached white bread flour, plus extra for dusting

2½ teaspoons sea salt

85 g unsalted butter, melted and cooled

3 medium eggs, beaten

vegetable oil, for greasing

1 egg yolk beaten with a pinch of salt, to glaze

a large baking sheet, greased

Makes 1 loaf

*To use easy-blend dried yeast, add one 7 g sachet to the flour with the salt and sugar, then proceed with the recipe.

A loaf with the distinctive taste of rye without the heavy texture – stoneground rye flour will produce the best flavour.

rye and caraway loaf

400 g unbleached white bread flour, plus extra for dusting

300 g rye flour

2 tablespoons caraway seeds

3 teaspoons sea salt

15 g fresh yeast, crumbled*

450 ml cold water

a baking sheet, greased

Makes 1 large loaf

*To use easy-blend dried yeast, mix one 7 g sachet with the flours, seeds and salt. Add the water and proceed with the recipe.

Put the two flours, caraway seeds and salt in a large bowl and mix. Make a well in the centre.

Put the yeast and a little of the water in a small bowl and cream to a smooth liquid. Pour this into the well in the flour with the rest of the water, then mix in the flour to make a soft but not sticky dough. If too sticky, add white flour, 1 tablespoon at a time. If there are dry crumbs in the bottom of the bowl and the dough is stiff and hard to work, add extra water, 1 tablespoon at a time.

Transfer the dough to a lightly floured work surface and knead thoroughly for 10 minutes. Return to the bowl, cover with a damp tea towel and let rise until doubled in size – about 2 hours.

Knock back the dough with your knuckles, then transfer to a lightly floured work surface. Knead lightly into an oval. With the edge of your hand, make a crease down the middle, then roll the dough over to make a sausage. Put the seam underneath so the top is smooth and evenly shaped. Place on the baking sheet, cover with a damp tea towel and let rise until doubled in size – about 1 hour.

Uncover the loaf and slash the top several times with a very sharp knife. Bake in a preheated oven at 200°C (400°F) Gas 6 for 15 minutes until golden, then reduce the oven temperature to 190°C (375°F) Gas 5 and bake for a further 20–25 minutes until the loaf sounds hollow when tapped underneath. Remove from the oven and transfer to a wire rack to cool.

chilli pepper bread

A mixed-flour loaf, speckled with dried chilli flakes.
Wonderful with smoked salmon and cream cheese – the
combination of hot, cold and savoury is irresistible.

Put the chilli flakes, flours and salt in a large bowl and mix. Put the yeast and
a little of the water in a small bowl and cream to a smooth paste.

Make a well in the flour mixture, pour in the yeast paste and the rest of the
water. Gradually work the flour into the liquid to make a soft but not sticky
dough. If it sticks to your hands, add a little more white flour. If there are dry
crumbs in the bowl and the dough is stiff and hard to work, add more water,
about 1 tablespoon at a time. Transfer to a lightly floured work surface and
knead for 10 minutes until very elastic and pliable. Return to the bowl, cover
with a damp tea towel and let rise at cool to normal room temperature until
doubled in size – about 2 hours.

Knock back the risen dough with your knuckles, then transfer to a lightly floured
work surface and shape to fit your tin. Put the dough in the tin and tuck under
the ends to make a neat shape (the top of the dough should be halfway
up the sides of the tin). Cover and leave at cool to normal room temperature
until the dough rises just above the rim of the tin – about 1½ hours.

Bake in a preheated oven at 230°C (450°F) Gas 8 for about 15 minutes. Reduce
the oven temperature to 200°C (400°F) Gas 6 and cook for 25–30 minutes
until the loaf sounds hollow when removed from the tin and tapped
underneath. Transfer to a wire rack to cool.

2–3 teaspoons dried chilli flakes
(the quantity depends on their
strength and your courage)

250 g strong white bread flour,
plus extra for dusting

250 g stoneground wholemeal
bread flour

250 g stoneground rye flour

3 teaspoons sea salt

15 g fresh yeast, crumbled*

450 ml water,
at room temperature

a loaf tin, 1 kg, greased

Makes 1 large loaf

*To use easy-blend dried yeast, mix
one 7 g sachet with the chilli flakes,
flours and salt. Add all the liquid at
once and proceed with the recipe.*

poppy seed loaf

A speckled, airy bread – great with soups and for making sandwiches.

Put the seeds, flour and salt in a large bowl and mix. Add the diced butter and rub it in with your fingertips until the mixture resembles fine crumbs. Stir in the sugar and make a well in the centre.

Put the yeast and a little of the milk in a small bowl and cream to a smooth liquid. Pour into the well in the flour with the egg and remaining milk.

Work the flour into the liquid to make a soft but not sticky dough. Transfer to a lightly floured work surface and knead thoroughly for 10 minutes. Return to the bowl, cover with a damp tea towel and let rise at cool to normal room temperature until doubled in size – 1½–2 hours.

Knock back the risen dough, then transfer to to a lightly floured work surface. Knead it smooth for 1 minute, then pat into a rectangle the length of the tin and about 1 cm thick. Roll up the dough like a Swiss roll from one short end. Pinch the seam with your fingers to seal, then put the dough into the tin, seam side down, tucking the ends underneath. The tin should be half filled. Cover with a damp tea towel and let rise at room temperature until doubled in size – about 1 hour.

Uncover, brush the top with milk and bake in a preheated oven at 230°C (450°F) Gas 8 for 15 minutes. Reduce the oven temperature to 200°C (400°F) Gas 6 and bake for 20–30 minutes until the loaf sounds hollow when removed from the tin and tapped underneath. Transfer to a wire rack to cool.

40 g poppy seeds

650 g unbleached white bread flour, plus extra for dusting

2 teaspoons sea salt

50 g unsalted butter, chilled and diced

1½ tablespoons golden caster sugar

15 g fresh yeast, crumbled*

375 ml skimmed milk, at room temperature, plus extra for brushing

1 medium egg, beaten

a loaf tin, 900 g, greased

Makes 1 large loaf

*To use easy-blend dried yeast, add one 7 g sachet to the flour with the salt and poppy seeds, then proceed with the recipe.

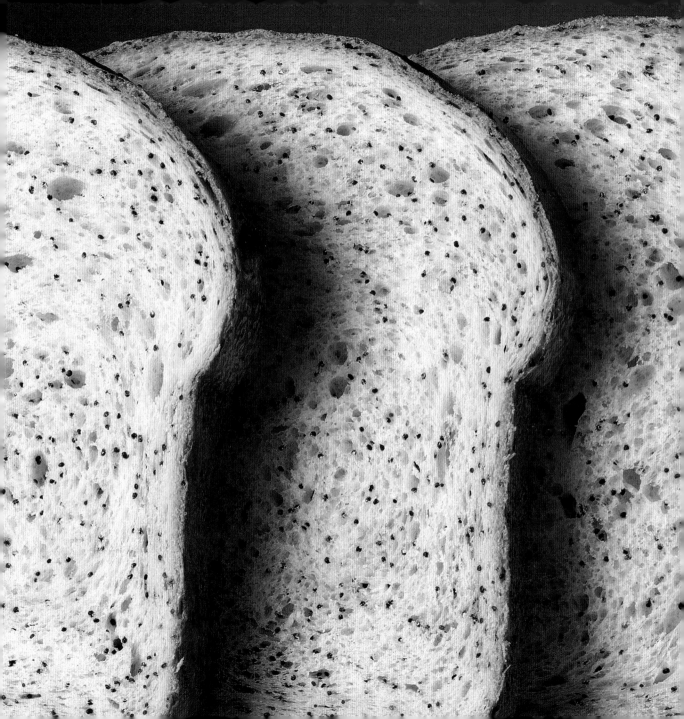

SPECIAL GRAINS

molasses mixed grain pumpernickel

250 g stoneground rye flour

150 g coarse wholemeal bread flour

100 g spelt flour

50 g barley flour

50 g buckwheat flour

100 g strong white bread flour, plus extra for dusting

50 g fine oatmeal

2 teaspoons sea salt

1½ tablespoons dark brown muscovado sugar

20 g fresh yeast, crumbled*

370 ml water

50 g molasses

1 tablespoon vegetable oil

a loaf tin, 900 g, greased

Makes 1 large loaf

*To use easy-blend dried yeast, mix 10 g (1½ x 7 g sachets) with the white flour. Put the other flours, salt and sugar in a bowl, make a well and add the water. Stir in the yeast and proceed with the recipe.

Put the flours, oatmeal, salt and sugar in a large bowl and mix. Make a well in the centre.

Put the yeast and a little of the water in a small bowl and cream to a smooth liquid. Stir in the rest of the water, then pour it into the well.

Mix some of the flour into the liquid in the well to make a thick, smooth batter. Sprinkle a little flour over the batter to prevent a skin forming, then cover and leave the bowl for 30 minutes until the batter looks bubbly.

Stir the molasses and oil into the batter, then gradually work in the rest of the flour to make a soft, slightly sticky dough. It will seem heavier and more difficult to work than other bread doughs, but if it is dry or too hard to work, you may need to add a little extra water, 1 tablespoon at a time. If it seems wet or too sticky, add a little extra white flour, 1 tablespoon at a time.

Transfer to a floured work surface and knead thoroughly for about 5 minutes. Cover the dough with an upturned bowl, let rest for about 5 minutes, then knead for a further 5 minutes. Return the dough to the bowl, cover with a damp tea towel and let rise at normal room temperature until doubled in size – about 3 hours .

Uncover, knock back the risen dough, then turn out on to a lightly floured work surface and knead for 1 minute. Shape the dough into a loaf to fit the tin, then put it in the tin, pushing it into the corners – the top of the dough should be halfway up the tin. Cover with a damp tea towel and let rise at normal room temperature until the dough reaches the top of the loaf tin – 1½–2 hours.

Bake in a preheated oven at 200°C (400°F) Gas 6 for about 40 minutes or until the loaf is dark brown and sounds hollow when removed from the tin and tapped underneath. Transfer to a wire rack to cool completely.

Keep wrapped in greaseproof paper for at least 1–2 days before slicing thinly. This loaf will mature when kept and will taste best about 4 days after baking.

VARIATION

Raisin Pumpernickel

Put 90 g of raisins or sultanas in a bowl, pour over enough orange juice to cover and let soak for about 1 hour. Drain, then add the fruit to the dough just before shaping into a loaf. Proceed as in the main recipe.

Molasses produces the traditional dark colour in this dense, rich bread made with a number of different flours, predominantly rye.

cheat's sourdough

Spelt flour has a nutty flavour and has recently become popular with organic farmers.

10 g fresh yeast, crumbled*

**600 ml water,
at room temperature**

550 g spelt flour

3 teaspoons sea salt

**about 350 g strong
white bread flour, plus extra
for dusting**

a large baking sheet, floured

Makes 1 large loaf

**I have had variable results with
easy-blend dried yeast and prefer
fresh yeast for this recipe.*

Put the yeast in a medium bowl with half the water and cream until smooth. Add 300 g spelt flour and stir to make a thick batter. Cover with a damp tea towel and set aside for 24 hours until it looks bubbly and slightly grey. Next day, stir in the remaining water to make a smooth batter. Transfer to a larger bowl, beat in the salt and remaining spelt flour with your hand, then gradually work in enough white flour to make a soft but not sticky dough (the amount depends on the quality of the spelt flour).

Transfer the dough to a floured work surface and knead for 10 minutes. If it sticks to your fingers, work in extra white flour, 1 tablespoon at a time. Return the dough to the bowl, cover with a damp tea towel and let rise at cool to normal room temperature until doubled in size – about 3 hours.

Uncover, knock back the dough, turn out on to a floured work surface and knead for 1 minute. It should be firm enough to hold its shape during baking; if too soft, work in extra flour.

Shape into a round loaf and put on the baking sheet. Cover loosely and let rise as before until almost doubled in size – 1½–2 hours. Uncover, then slash the top several times with a very sharp knife. Sprinkle with white flour, then bake in a preheated oven at 220°C (425°F) Gas 7 for 20 minutes. Reduce the oven temperature to 200°C (400°F) Gas 6 and bake for 15 minutes or until the loaf sounds hollow when tapped underneath. Remove from the oven and transfer to a wire rack to cool.

wholemeal beer bread

400 g stoneground wholemeal bread flour

100 g coarsely ground wholemeal bread flour or wheaten bread flour, plus extra for dusting

2 teaspoons sea salt

15 g fresh yeast, crumbled*

1 tablespoon lukewarm water

about 350 ml beer, at room temperature

a baking sheet, greased

Makes 1 medium loaf

*To use easy-blend dried yeast, add one 7 g sachet to the flour, then proceed with the recipe. Omit the water and add 1 extra tablespoon beer.

Put the flours and salt in a large bowl and mix. Make a well in the centre. Put the yeast and water in a small bowl and cream to a smooth paste.

Add the yeast paste and the beer to the well in the flour. Mix to a soft but not sticky dough, working it for several minutes before adding anything else.

The amount of liquid you need will depend on the flour, but the dough will feel very different from a white bread dough. If it seems very wet, add extra flour, 1 tablespoon at a time. If stiff and dry, with dry crumbs in the bottom of the bowl, work in extra beer or water, 1 tablespoon at a time.

Transfer the dough to a floured work surface and knead for 5–7 minutes until the dough is smooth and pliable. Return to the bowl, cover with a damp cloth and let rise at normal room temperature until doubled in size – about 2 hours.

Knock back the risen dough and shape into a ball. Put on the baking sheet, cover loosely with a damp tea towel and let rise again as before until doubled in size – about 1 hour.

Uncover the loaf, slash the top with a very sharp knife, sprinkle with coarsely ground wholemeal flour and bake in a preheated oven at 220°C (425°F) Gas 7 for 30–35 minutes until the loaf is golden brown and sounds hollow when tapped underneath. Remove from the oven and transfer to a wire rack to cool.

German smoked beer, brown ale or stout give deepest flavour: pale ale a more subtle taste.

FRUIT & NUTS

honeynut loaf

350 g stoneground wholemeal bread flour

350 g unbleached white bread flour, plus extra for dusting

2½ teaspoons sea salt

20 g fresh yeast, crumbled*

350 ml water, at room temperature

3 tablespoons well-flavoured honey

300 g nuts (any combination of walnuts, hazelnuts, almonds, cashews or macadamias), lightly toasted and roughly chopped

2 baking sheets, greased

Makes 2 medium loaves

*To use easy-blend dried yeast, mix one 7 g sachet with the flour and salt, add the water and honey, then proceed with the recipe.

Put the flours and salt in a large bowl, mix, then make a well in the centre.

Put the yeast and a little of the water in a small bowl and cream to a smooth liquid. Pour this mixture into the well in the flour.

Dissolve the honey in the rest of the water and add it to the well. Gradually work the flour into the liquid to make a soft but not sticky dough. If the dough sticks to your fingers, work in extra flour, about 1 tablespoon at a time. If there are dry crumbs in the bottom of the bowl, or the dough seems stiff and hard to work, add extra water, 1 tablespoon at a time.

Transfer the dough to a lightly floured work surface and knead thoroughly for 10 minutes until smooth and elastic.

Flatten the dough with your hand, sprinkle about one third of the nuts over the dough, then fold it over and over to mix them.

Repeat this process twice more, then shape the dough into a ball and return it to the bowl.

Cover with a damp tea towel and let rise at cool to normal room temperature until doubled in size – about 2 hours.

Uncover, knock back the risen dough with your knuckles, then turn out on to a floured work surface and knead for 1 minute to ensure the nuts are evenly distributed.

Divide the dough in half. Shape each portion into a neat ball, pushing back any nuts that protrude or escape.

Put the balls of dough on a baking sheet, cover as before and let rise at cool to normal room temperature until doubled in size – about 1½ hours.

Uncover the loaves and slash the tops diagonally several times with a very sharp knife. Bake in a preheated oven at 220°C (425°F) Gas 7 for about 15 minutes, then reduce the oven temperature to 190°C (375°F) Gas 5 and bake for a further 20–25 minutes.

The loaves should sound hollow when removed from the baking sheet and tapped underneath. Transfer to a wire rack to cool.

VARIATION

New England Maple Nut Loaf

A wonderful combination of traditional American ingredients – dried cranberries, maple syrup and pecan nuts.

Omit the roasted nuts from the main recipe and add 75 g dried cranberries and 150 g pecan nuts broken into pieces. Substitute 3 tablespoons maple syrup for the honey, and proceed as in the main recipe.

Make this well-flavoured bread, loaded with nuts, with a mixture of flours and a pungent honey, such as heather. Use any combination of nuts, but for the best taste they should be lightly toasted. Serve with butter, cream cheese or cheese.

Use a good sugarless muesli with ingredients such as raisins, dates, wheat flakes, oat flakes, apples, apricots, hazelnuts, almonds and raisins.

muesli round

Put the flours, muesli and salt in a large bowl and mix well. Make a well in the centre.

Put the yeast and 3 tablespoons of the milk in a small bowl and cream to a smooth liquid. Stir in the rest of the liquid, the honey and oil, then pour into the well in the flour.

Gradually mix the dry ingredients into the liquid to make a fairly firm dough. If it seems dry or stiff, or there are dry crumbs in the bottom of the bowl, work in extra milk or water, 1 tablespoon at a time. If the dough sticks to your fingers, knead in extra white flour, 1 tablespoon at a time. The amount of liquid needed will depend on the muesli mix.

Transfer the dough to a lightly floured work surface and knead for about 5 minutes. Return the dough to the bowl, cover with a damp tea towel and leave at room temperature until doubled in size – 1–1½ hours. Turn out on to a lightly floured work surface and knead for 1 minute. Shape into a round loaf 20 cm across. Put on the prepared baking sheet and score into 8 segments with a very sharp knife. Cover and let rise as before – for about 1 hour.

Uncover the loaf and sprinkle with wholemeal flour. Cook in a preheated oven at 220°C (425°F) Gas 7 for 30 minutes or until it sounds hollow when tapped underneath. Remove from the oven and transfer to a wire rack to cool.

500 g strong white bread flour

100 g stoneground wholemeal flour, plus extra for dusting

250 g unsweetened muesli

2 teaspoons salt

15 g fresh yeast, crumbled*

about 400 ml milk and water mixed, at room temperature

1 tablespoon honey

2 tablespoons vegetable oil

a baking sheet, greased

Makes 1 large round loaf

*To use easy-blend dried yeast, mix one 7 g sachet with the two kinds of flour, the muesli and salt. Pour in all the liquids, then proceed with the recipe.

blue cheese and walnut twist

300 g unbleached white bread flour, plus extra for dusting

1 teaspoon sea salt

40 g butter, chilled and diced

10 g fresh yeast, crumbled*

50 ml milk mixed with 50 ml water, at room temperature

1 medium egg, beaten

Blue Cheese and Walnut Filling

200 g cream cheese

1 tablespoon milk

50 g finely ground walnuts

125 g blue cheese

125 g walnut pieces

freshly ground black pepper

a baking sheet, greased

Makes 1 loaf

To use easy-blend dried yeast, mix 2 teaspoons with the flour and salt, then proceed with the recipe.

Put the flour and salt in a large bowl and mix. Add the butter and rub it in with your fingertips until the mixture looks like fine crumbs. Make a well in the centre.

Put the yeast and the milk and water in a small bowl and cream until smooth. Mix in the egg, then pour into the well in the flour. Gradually work in the flour to make a soft but not sticky dough.

Transfer to a floured work surface and knead for 10 minutes until smooth, silky and elastic. Return the dough to the bowl, cover with a damp tea towel and let rise at normal room temperature until doubled in size – about 1 hour.

To make the filling, beat the cream cheese and milk until soft, then beat in the ground walnuts and black pepper. In a separate bowl, crumble the blue cheese into small chunks, add the walnut pieces and mix.

Uncover the risen dough and knock back, then roll out on a lightly floured work surface into a rectangle about 33 x 30 cm. Spread the cream cheese mixture over the top, then scatter with blue cheese and walnuts.

Roll up the dough fairly tightly from one long side, like a Swiss roll, then roll this into a longer, thinner cylinder about 60 cm long. Cut in half lengthways with a sharp knife. Twist the halves together, cut sides up, and shape into a neat ring on the baking sheet.

Cover loosely with a damp tea towel and let rise at room temperature until doubled in size – 45–60 minutes.

Bake in a preheated oven at 200°C (400°F) Gas 6 for 25 minutes or until firm and golden. Remove from the oven and transfer to a wire rack to cool.

sour cherry loaf

A flavourful loaf, not too sweet – good with cold meat and pickles.

350 g unbleached white bread flour, plus extra for dusting

150 g rye flour, stoneground if possible

80 g dried sour cherries

2 teaspoons sea salt

15 g fresh yeast, crumbled*

about 300 ml cold water

a baking sheet, greased

Makes 1 medium loaf

*To use easy-blend dried yeast, add one 7 g sachet to the flour, then proceed with the recipe.

Put the flours, dried sour cherries and salt in a large bowl, mix, then make a well in the centre. Put the yeast and half the water in a small bowl and cream until smooth. Pour into the well in the flour, add the remaining water, then gradually mix in the flour to make a soft but not sticky dough. If it seems sticky and difficult to work, mix in white flour, 1 tablespoon at a time. If stiff and dry, with crumbs in the bottom of the bowl, work in water, 1 tablespoon at a time (the amount of liquid needed will depend on the quality of the flour).

Transfer the dough to a lightly floured work surface and knead for about 10 minutes until satiny and elastic. Return the dough to the bowl, cover with a damp tea towel and let rise at cool to normal room temperature until doubled in size – about 2 hours.

Uncover the dough, knock back and turn out on to a lightly floured work surface. Gently knead into an oval. With the edge of your hand, make a crease down the middle, then roll the dough over to make a sausage shape about 25 cm long. Place, seam side down, on the baking sheet. Cover as before and let rise at normal room temperature until doubled in size – about 1 hour.

Uncover and slash the loaf several times across the top with a very sharp knife. Bake in a preheated oven at 220°C (425°F) Gas 7 for 15 minutes until golden. Reduce the oven temperature to 190°C (375°F) Gas 5 and bake for 10–15 minutes until the loaf sounds hollow when tapped underneath. Remove from the oven and transfer to a wire rack to cool.

VEGETABLES
& CHEESE

garlic knots

Roasted garlic produces a delicious aroma with no harsh taste.

500 g strong white bread flour, plus extra for dusting

1½ teaspoons sea salt

10 g fresh yeast, crumbled*

300 ml cold water

1 tablespoon virgin olive oil

12 unpeeled garlic cloves

a pinch of salt

1 egg beaten with a good pinch of salt, to glaze

2 baking sheets, greased

Makes 12

*To use easy-blend dried yeast, mix 5 g (⅔ x 7 g sachet) with the flour and salt. Proceed with the recipe.

Put the flour and salt in a large bowl and make a well in the centre. Put the yeast and a little of the water in a small bowl and cream until smooth. Stir in the oil and the remaining water, then pour into the well in the flour. Work in the flour to make a soft but not sticky dough. If too sticky, work in extra flour, 1 tablespoon at a time. If there are dry crumbs in the bowl, work in extra water, 1 tablespoon at a time.

Turn the dough out on to a floured work surface and knead for 10 minutes until smooth, silky and elastic. Return to the bowl, cover with a damp tea towel and let rise at cool to normal room temperature until doubled in size – 1½–2 hours .

Put the garlic in a roasting tin and cook in a preheated oven at 190°C (375°F) Gas 5 for 10 minutes until the skin is split and golden and the flesh soft and ripe smelling. Let cool, then peel, sprinkle with salt and mash into a rough paste with the back of a knife.

Uncover the dough, knock back, then divide into 12 equal pieces. Shape each piece into a sausage 20 cm long and flatten slightly. Spread the garlic paste on the top, then tie into knots. Place well apart on the baking sheets, cover with a damp tea towel and let rise until doubled in size – about 45 minutes.

Brush with the egg glaze, then bake in a preheated oven at 220°C (425°F) Gas 7 for 10–15 minutes until golden brown and sound hollow when tapped underneath. Remove from the oven and transfer to a wire rack to cool.

onion rolls

Slow-cooked onion and rye flour give flavour without pungency.

Put the onion, sugar and butter in a heavy saucepan and heat gently, stirring, until soft and slightly caramelized. Let cool.

Put the flours and salt in a bowl, mix, then make a well in the centre. Put the yeast and a little water in a small bowl and cream until smooth. Pour into the well in the flour and add the onion and remaining water. Work in the flour to make a soft but not sticky dough. If it sticks to your fingers or the bowl, work in extra white flour, 1 tablespoon at a time. If it seems stiff, with dry crumbs in the bowl, slowly work in extra water, 1 tablespoon at a time.

Turn out the dough on to a floured work surface and knead for 10 minutes until very smooth and elastic. Return to the bowl, cover with a damp tea towel and let rise at cool to normal room temperature until doubled in size – 1–1½ hours.

Uncover the dough and knock back. Turn out on to a floured work surface and knead for 1 minute. Weigh and divide into 14 equal pieces. Shape into balls and place well apart on the baking sheets.

To make the onion shapes, pinch the centres, drawing them up to make a stalk. Cover with a damp tea towel – to avoid flattening the stalks, use upturned bowls to support the towel. Let rise for 30 minutes, until doubled in size.

Brush with the egg glaze, then bake in a preheated oven at 220°C (425°F) Gas 7 for 15–20 minutes until shiny golden brown. Remove from the oven and transfer to a wire rack to cool.

1 large onion, finely chopped

½ teaspoon caster sugar

25 g unsalted butter

400 g strong white bread flour, plus extra for dusting

100 g rye flour, preferably stoneground

2½ teaspoons sea salt

15 g fresh yeast, crumbled*

300 ml water, at room temperature

1 egg beaten with a pinch of salt, to glaze

2 baking sheets, greased

Makes 14

*To use easy-blend dried yeast, mix one 7 g sachet with the flours and salt, add the water and onion mixture, then proceed with the recipe.

Pumpkin makes a fine, soft, golden
bread that toasts well.

pumpkin bread

Peel the pumpkin or other squash and remove the seeds. Dice the flesh into
1 cm cubes – you will need 400 g in total.

Without adding water, cook the cubes in a steamer or microwave until they
soften. Put them in a food processor with the oil and process until smooth.
Let cool until just lukewarm, then mix in the salt and sugar.

Put the yeast and lukewarm water in a small bowl and cream to a smooth
paste. Mix the paste into the pumpkin purée.

Put the flour in a large bowl and make a well in the centre. Spoon the purée
into the well, then mix in the flour to make a soft but not sticky dough. Turn
out on to a floured work surface and knead thoroughly for 5 minutes (or
3 minutes at low speed in a mixer with a dough hook).

Shape the dough into a round loaf about 18 cm across and put it on the
baking sheet. Cover with a damp tea towel and let rise at normal room
temperature until doubled in size – about 1½ hours.

Press your thumb into the middle of the risen loaf to make a small hollow,
then carefully brush the loaf with the egg glaze. Score the loaf into segments
with a very sharp knife, then bake in a preheated oven at 200°C (400°F) Gas 6
for about 30 minutes until it is golden brown and sounds hollow when tapped
underneath. Remove from the oven and transfer to a wire rack to cool.

**700 g pumpkin, Japanese
kabocha or other winter squash**

1 tablespoon virgin olive oil

2½ teaspoons sea salt

2 teaspoons golden caster sugar

15 g fresh yeast, crumbled*

1 tablespoon lukewarm water

**350 g strong white bread flour,
plus extra for dusting**

**1 egg beaten with a pinch of salt,
to glaze**

a baking sheet, greased

Makes 1 medium loaf

**To use easy-blend dried yeast, mix
one 7 g sachet with the flour, then
work in the pumpkin purée. If the
dough seems dry or there are dry
crumbs in the bottom of the bowl,
work in a little cold water.*

easy cheese brioche

A rich, light, tangy loaf – and easily made in a mixer, unlike
a classic brioche. Serve it with cheese, salad or soup.

Crumble the yeast into the bowl of a free-standing mixer. Pour in the milk
and mix with the whisk attachment. Whisk in the eggs, then the salt and
cayenne pepper.

Using the dough hook at low speed, gradually work in the flour to make
a soft but not sticky dough. Knead in the machine at low speed for another
5 minutes until smooth and elastic.

Add the softened butter and knead for another 3–4 minutes until completely
mixed. Cover with a damp tea towel and let rise at normal room temperature
until doubled in size – about 1½ hours.

Knead the grated cheese into the dough for about 1 minute at slow speed,
then turn out on to a floured work surface and shape into a loaf to fit the tin.

Put the dough in the tin, then cover with a damp tea towel and leave at
normal room temperature until doubled in size – about 1 hour (the dough
should just reach the rim of the tin).

Gently brush the risen loaf with egg glaze, taking care not to glue it to the
sides of the tin.

Sprinkle with the extra cheese and bake in a preheated oven at 200°C (400°F)
Gas 6 for about 35 minutes until it turns golden brown and sounds hollow
when turned out of the tin and tapped underneath. Remove from the oven
and transfer to a wire rack to cool.

15 g fresh yeast*

100 ml lukewarm skimmed milk

2 medium eggs

1 teaspoon sea salt

¼ teaspoon cayenne pepper

**300 g strong white bread flour,
plus extra for dusting**

50 g unsalted butter, softened

**100 g Gruyère cheese, grated,
plus 25 g extra, to finish**

**1 egg beaten with a large pinch
of salt, to glaze**

a loaf tin, 500 g, greased

Makes 1 medium loaf

**To use easy-blend dried yeast, mix
one 7 g sachet with the flour and
work into the liquids in the bowl.
Proceed with the recipe.*

cheese baps with cheddar and onion

650 g unbleached white bread flour, plus extra for dusting

2 teaspoons sea salt

1 teaspoon mustard powder

200 g mature Cheddar cheese, grated

40 g spring onions, finely chopped

15 g fresh yeast, crumbled*

200 ml skimmed milk, at room temperature, plus extra for glazing

200 ml water, at room temperature

vegetable oil, for greasing

2 baking sheets, lightly greased

Makes 12

*To use easy-blend dried yeast, add one 7 g sachet to the flour, then proceed with the recipe.

Put the flour, salt, mustard powder, 150 g Cheddar and spring onions in a large bowl and mix. Make a well in the centre.

Put the yeast and the milk in a small bowl and cream to a smooth liquid. Stir in the water, then pour into the well in the flour. Gradually work the flour into the liquid to make a soft but not sticky dough.

Turn out the dough on to a floured work surface and knead for 10 minutes until it feels smooth and elastic. It can also be kneaded for 5 minutes at low speed in a mixer fitted with a dough hook. Put the dough into a lightly greased bowl, turning it so the entire surface is lightly coated with oil. Cover with a damp tea towel and let rise until doubled in size – 1½–2 hours.

Uncover the dough, knock back, then turn out on to a floured work surface and knead for a few seconds. Divide the dough into 12 equal parts and pat into ovals about 11 x 8 x 3 cm. Arrange well apart on the baking sheets. Brush with milk, then sprinkle with the remaining Cheddar. Let rise until doubled in size – about 30 minutes.

Press your thumb into the middle of each bap, then bake in a preheated oven at 220°C (425°F) Gas 7 for 15 minutes until golden. Remove from the oven and transfer to a wire rack to cool.

For the best flavour, use mature cheese: much so-called Cheddar is too bland for this recipe.

index

credits

All photographs by **Patrice de Villiers** unless otherwise stated.

Martin Brigdale Endpapers, pages 1 above left, 2, 4, 7 centre left & centre right, 8–9, 10, 13, 27, 29 left, 35, 39 centre, 43, 49 centre and right, 59, 62, 67–70, 72, 73, 83, 89, 101 centre, 107, 113 left & centre, 129 centre, 139 left & centre, 144, 180–1, 182, 185 centre, 196, 119, 203, 209, 215, 217 centre, 227 left, 240

Peter Cassidy Pages 1 above right, 7 right, 101 right, 113 right, 159 centre & right, 185 left & right, 197, 227 centre

Debi Treloar Pages 5, 29 centre & right, 39 left & right, 49 left, 126, 145 right

Nicky Dowey Pages 7 left, 171 right, 217 right

Vanessa Davies Page 129 right, 171 centre

Jean Cazals Page 145 left

Christine Hanscomb Page 6

Jeremy Hopley Page 217 left

William Lingwood Pages 124–5

David Munns Page 227 right

Craig Robertson Page 159 left

Ian Wallace Page 101 left